SCALING the Scholarship Mountain

Achieving Scholarly Productivity

By Charlie Sweet, Hal Blythe,
Russell Carpenter & Bill Phillips

NEW FORUMS PRESS INC.

Published in the United States of America
by New Forums Press, Inc. 1018 S. Lewis St.
Stillwater, OK 74074
www.newforums.com

Copyright © 2017 by New Forums Press, Inc.

All rights reserved. No part of this publication may be reproduced or transmitted in any form or by any means, electronic or mechanical, including photocopy, or any information storage or retrieval system, without permission in writing from the publisher.

Library of Congress Cataloging-in-Publication Data Pending

This book may be ordered in bulk quantities at discount from New Forums Press, Inc., P.O. Box 876, Stillwater, OK 74076 [Federal I.D. No. 73 1123239]. Printed in the United States of America.

ISBN 10: 1-58107-303-8
ISBN 13: 978-1-58107-303-4

Table of Contents

Preface v

1. Preparing for the Climb **1**

    I. Introduction 3

    II. Why Produce Scholarship, Why Right Now? 7

    III. Defining a Scholarly Frame of Mind 11

    IV. Taking Inventory 17

    V. Analyzing the Market 21

    VI. Becoming a Disciplined Scholar Using SOARS Guidelines 27

    VII. Utilizing Boyer's Understanding of Scholarly Mountains 35

    VIII. The Importance of SoTL 41

2. Beginning the Ascent **49**

    IX. Generating Ideas 51

    X. Following the Trail of the Typical Article 59

3. Into Thin Air **65**

    XI. Collaboration with Colleagues and Students 67

    XII. Charting Your Way with Multiple Projects 75

    XIII. Overcoming Other Obstacles 81

    XIV. A Checklist for Starting Your Scholarly Project 91

About the Authors 93

PREFACE

When Bill finished his doctorate in education and began applying for jobs, one advertisement in the *Chronicle of Higher Education* puzzled him. The ad asked for evidence of scholarly productivity. He thought, what is "scholarly productivity" and how does one achieve it?

Only years later did Bill develop a metacognitive awareness that a definite process to becoming a scholar existed and what those key components were. The process involved reading, studying, critical thinking, learning, application of knowledge, teaching, and writing, all of which Bill had experienced beginning as early as K-12 and continuing through undergraduate work, graduate research (especially his dissertation), and his early years of teaching. Even so, the climb from his formal training to scholarly productivity seemed daunting.

Slowly, however, Bill learned how to identify current trends, do a literature review on a current topic, synthesize the writing of others, and add his perspective. Putting his thoughts on paper resulted in proposals for presentations that were accepted at local, regional, national, and international conferences. The conferences often provided an opportunity to publish conference proceedings and always provided feedback from attendees. By attending these conferences, Bill was able to visit with other professionals and learn from them. The conference proceedings led to articles that were peer reviewed and published in journals. The literature reviews, presentations, proceedings, and articles opened the door for publishing books.

This book is intended to aid you in the climb from your formal education experience to the real world of the scholar. Through a combined total of over 150 years of experience in scholarly productivity, the authors have discovered some key steps toward becoming a scholar. In the pages that follow, they will share these steps through explanations, examples, and exercises.

Since we have also edited several publications in the past, and Rusty currently serves as editor of the prestigious *Journal of Faculty Development*, we had decided to include a special section in this book to further aid you in scaling the scholarship mountain. "From the Editor's Desk" Post 'Ems are timely observations made in reference to important concepts introduced in the text. Each comment is designed to call attention to a specific point, establishing its place in the successful ascent to scholarly productivity.

Charlie Sweet, Hal Blythe, Russell Carpenter, & Bill Phillips

1

Preparing for the Climb

I. INTRODUCTION

When Charlie took his first job out of grad school, his new chair gave him some simple guidelines: in your first year be the best teacher you can be, and, after that, publish one item per year. Charlie dedicated his first year to the classroom, but in the back of his head he was developing an idea he had come up with while teaching in grad school. His second year he continued to teach as well as he could, but wrote an article on Edwin Arlington Robinson's "Richard Cory" and published it in a journal from Robinson's home state, the *Colby Library Quarterly*.

Cut to the present. As the author's bio on the cover of this book proclaims, Charlie has 25 books and over 1200 publications. How did he go from a single publication to so many? Incrementally. Actually, Charlie went to a graduate school that emphasized publishing. In fact, one time at a South Atlantic Modern Language Association meeting in Atlanta while he was still a grad student, the chair of his department looked over a cocktail and offered some great advice. "Charlie," he said, "there's not a school in America you can't write your way into . . . or out of." So while in grad school Charlie developed a publishing mentality, having his short stories appear in two magazines and even selling an article to *TV Guide*.

What Charlie learned early in his career is a pathway to scholarly productivity we called in our previous books for New Forums on research and scholarship—*It Works for Me as a Scholar-Teacher* (2008) and *It Works for Me: Becoming a Publishing Scholar/Researcher* (2010)—climbing the publishing staircase. In the last couple of years, however, working with colleagues at our university, discussing issues with scholars from across the country, and editing various journals and scholarly collections have revealed that **scholarly production is a long, difficult task, more like scaling a mountain than merely climbing a staircase.** As a result, we have included several concerns and strategies in this book that we haven't previously considered. Here, we pay more attention to each aspect of preparing, revising, and "marketing" as you make your assent toward the peak.

This recognition is the first step in achieving your goal!

While this book primarily targets the newly-minted professor, its basic strategies are appropriate for anyone wishing to make the difficult climb. Charlie captured the sense of academic drive necessary in a poem he published in *College English* (1974):

THE ASSISTANT PROFESSOR

> Like an anxious octopus
> Who fills the depths with black fluid
> When scared I smear
> Ebony ink on white paper
> My two arms becoming eight
> Nightly slithering towards tenure.

Indeed, tenure and higher pay may be the strongest motivators for scholarly productivity, but they are not the only benefits you can derive from engaging in the scholarly life.

What this book offers that is different from other sources is that while it starts with the simpler concerns and strategies for the novice climber, it progresses through the stages to the more complex climbs. Beginners start on climbing boards, progress to walls at a health club, move up to local peaks, and later in their careers attack the Mount Everests of the publishing world.

We love both Boice's *Professors as Writers: A Self-Help Guide to Productive Writing* (1990) and Tara Gray's *Publish & Flourish: Become a Prolific Scholar* (2005), but they are both aimed at the non-writer in academia and the beginner. Our *It Works for Me as a Scholar-Teacher* (2008) and *It Works for Me: Becoming a Publishing Scholar-Researcher* (2010) target both the beginner and the intermediary stage. An Internet search "Tips for Academic Publishing" results in a series of books and articles condensing the academic writing process into "25 Tips for Breaking into Academic Publishing," "5 Tips . . .," "Ten Publishing Tips . . .," even "30 tips." All of the aforementioned sources, including ours, lack the rigor and complexity necessary to achieve the highest level of scholarly productivity.

This book covers the entire gamut from novice to expert, from Lunch-`n-Learn presentations to one's home department to the lead article in *PMLA* and those other K-2s of the publishing world, books. Furthermore, this book will even provide complex organizational charts to help you make the climb. In a recent post in the *Chronicle of Higher Education* on "The Trick to Being a Prolific Scholar," the author established her writing chops by noting she has just submitted her fifth book proposal for publication. Hal and Charlie alone have 25 books and over 1200 articles in print, so you can trust we have the experience to be your guides.

Why Do Scholarship?

Clarity of thought. Writing something down is often the best way to figure out exactly what you mean. Have you ever come out of class and realized you weren't exactly clear in

With writing comes clarity.

how you answered a student's question? Joan Didion claims, "I don't know what to think until I write it down," and Flannery O'Connor echoes this notion with, "I write because I don't know what I think until I read what I say." "How do I know what I think until I see what I say?" is E. M. Forster's expression of the same thought. Writing provides a form for filtering out the lint in fuzzy thinking. Hemingway once advised a young writer to pen a million words and then he would be ready to write, but was a little more graphic in what one had to evacuate from the body to achieve clarity. As with these masters of fiction, you can gain great clarity concerning your ideas through researching, then actually writing down your findings for reflection and assessment by others.

Scholarly productivity takes time and focused effort!

Self-motivation. One thing all four of us have in common as successful writers is the compulsion to write. We all write in part because we can't not write. We write copious emails, lots of tweets, letters to old friends, and even notes to ourselves on what to write. On the day, for instance, that this piece is being written, we finished proofing the galleys for our latest academic book, and we spent the morning printing out a novel. All of us have achieved tenure, so while we don't have to continue to write, we choose to. As you climb ever closer to the mountaintop, refining your scholarly approach with each step, you'll find that you become more motivated, more excited about possibilities. You'll be no more willing or able to miss your scholarly time than a meal.

Development of writing expertise. Ericsson's theory of deliberate practice posits that **in order to achieve expertise in any field from playing basketball to playing in a rock band, one needs 10,000 hours or ten years of deliberate practice.** Hemingway's one-million words. In college and grad school, the average professor, despite a dissertation, does not come close to picking up the necessary hours to become an expert writer. In *Academically Adrift* (2011) Arum and Roksa point out that the absence of 40-page papers—i.e, extensive writing—prevents college students from developing as writers. We write and rate each other's writing so that we all improve. Years ago, Hal and Charlie had a graduate student who constantly came up with what he believed to be brilliant literary insights. Try as they might, however, they could never get their student to research, write out, and submit his ideas for publication. So many excellent insights withered on the vine because Ben refused to join the scholarly conversation.

An old Hollywood axiom states that "Nothing is written—everything is rewritten." Scholarly activity demands that you sharpen your communication through writing, review, critique (by you and others), and revision. **With each rewrite, you become a stronger writer.** Bill is a perfect example. Burdened with dyslexia, Bill began as a poor writer, but he was willing to keep trying and submit his prose to accomplished writers, who mentored him. As a result, Bill has turned a weakness into a strength.

Deep learning. In our first two books in New Forums' Innovations in Faculty Development series—*Achieving Excellence in Teaching* (2014) and *Transforming Your Students into Deep Learners* (2016)—we provide a detailed strategy designed to 1) allow you to develop the most effective pedagogical approach possible and 2) give you the tools to help your students bridge "the learning gap" between surface and deep learning. Our research and writing for those texts led us to a realization of the important role scholarship plays in both the development of solid classroom pedagogy and the fostering of deep learning in students.

Achieve focus through revision!

Perhaps the most important function scholarship performs for a teacher is a transformation in its own right: from a static sage content to rehash material semester after semester to an active model for students, constantly challenging the status quo with fresh ideas and a willingness to share those ideas for critical review. With this transformation comes an invaluable bonus as the teacher becomes through the scholarly process a deep learner, open to new knowledge in both teaching and learning.

With its advice, evidence, and exercises, this book offers you the opportunity for deliberate practice. If you follow Roethke's advice, "I learn by going where I have to go," you will learn, but you will also take a lot of needless paths upon which you may be learning, but learning the wrong things, things that can hinder your development as a scholar. This book will offer you expert assistance in scaling the scholarship mountain, helping you ascend one face at a time. Remember, you came out of grad school a content expert, not a publishing scholar.

If you have had a mentor, you know how valuable one can be. If you haven't had a mentor, you have probably expended a lot of extra time and energy and made too many false starts. In either case, **this book will function as a mentor, helping you form a scholarly plan, execute it, and deal with the many obstacles in your path.**

References

Boice, R. (1990). *Professors as writers.* Stillwater, OK: New Forums Press.

Gray, T. (2005). *Publish & Flourish.* Las Cruces, NM: Teaching Academy.

II. WHY PRODUCE SCHOLARSHIP, WHY RIGHT NOW?

In the previous chapter, we started with the story of Charlie's being told by the department head who hired him to concentrate on teaching the first year and publishing in subsequent years. That was over 40 years ago. If Charlie heeded that advice now as a new hire or even proclaimed it as a chair to a new hire of his, he would be consigned/consigning a new faculty member to failure. Bill, who served as a dean for fourteen years, used to recommend that all of the new faculty hired in his college (Education) be given reassigned time their very first semester, partially to help them adapt to the demands of scholarship.

In today's higher education climate, you have only a short window to produce before you are gone. Most institutions grant tenure and promotion after five or six years (the five was the norm when Charlie first came into academia). However, the competition is fiercer. The field of English now has grad schools produce two people for every position. With there no longer being a mandatory retirement age and tough economic times, senior professors are reluctant to retire, also decreasing the number of professorial slots. With the increased supply and still a steady demand, most departments don't worry much about letting someone go. In fact, if your second-year report doesn't indicate sufficient progress toward publication, you may find the window shut early.

The law of supply and demand affects publications and publishers, too. With the tenure stakes raised, the available markets are saturated with manuscripts. Many have a backlog and are frankly refusing to read any more manuscripts until the previous ones have been considered/published. Even previously moderately competitive journals are receiving higher volumes of submissions. Hard economic times have forced libraries, the principal buyer of academic texts, to cut back or even fold.

Some graduate schools recognize the pressure and therefore are teaching their students how to write publishable manuscripts. Thirty years ago Hal and Charlie were teaching college juniors how to write publishable scholarly notes, and their students were flooding the marketplace with notes good enough to get published. In fact, one semester one of Charlie's Am Lit classes had more notes published than did the rest of the English department. More manuscripts and fewer publication slots mean a decreased chance of getting published.

Why, you might ask, is there such an emphasis today on publishing? In an ideal world it's part of the holy trinity of responsibilities—teaching, scholarship and service—but it has assumed a larger role in recent years. We could argue it's a manifestation of scholarly teaching, but the truth is, after sitting on numerous promotion and tenure committees, we found scholarship/research is much easier to quantify than either teaching or service. Evaluation of effective teaching demands a trained observer with sufficient experience, but despite its rubrics and other rigor, teaching assessment is still highly subjective. Service, on the other hand, is quantifiable in the sense that anyone can provide the number of hours worked on a civic project, but determining the quality of such work is difficult. Professor X might sit on several university committees and an equal number of community boards, but how much work did the good professor do and what quality?

Scholarship is highly quantifiable—and objective. Most departments examine all the types of publication in their field from book reviews to blog posts to full-length books and establish a rubric that rates all the possibilities on a scale. Ah, you have two books with prestigious publishers, one peer-reviewed article in a tier one publication—oh, that's a 12. Committees and administrators, fearful of being sued for their subjective judgments that might be biased in some fashion, resort to the scholarship numerical rating. Objectivity is the stay against a legal backlash.

> Scholarship CAN be measured more objectively.

Now let's consider the newbie thrown into teaching three new preps. Between your reading for class prep, your creation of PowerPoints and videos, your grading of tests and quizzes, your office hours, your answering emails and checking on social media, your serving on committees such as faculty senate that your colleagues don't want, your entering grades in a Learning Management System (LMS), your attempt to attend at least one event at your center for teaching and learning, and your presence at both the department poetry slam and university homecoming game, how much scholarship are you accomplishing?

The first year of teaching is the hardest you will ever have. And that's true of many first-yearlings in a new field. Consider new law firm associates trying to manage 90 billable hours per week, and you might think you have it easy. Years ago Hal and Charlie had an office on the same floor as a new hire, Chad. Chad liked their coffee, loved to chat, and hated his entire newbie experience. Chad spent most of his chat time griping about some inane policy or inaner student. When he rarely talked about scholarship, he uttered the magi-

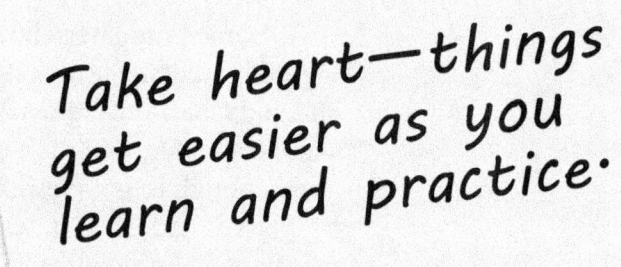

> Take heart—things get easier as you learn and practice.

cal word "Trope" as though Harry Potter were waving a wand to get things done. But Chad never got anything done. He never wrote his first article, stayed behind in his grading, led the grapevine league in grumbling words, and after three years disappeared from sight. Bill had similar experiences with colleagues who never managed to publish anything and never found a mentor to help them climb the scholarship mountain.

Before you start singing a chorus of "Na na na na, na na na na, hey, hey, hey, goodbye," consider what the Chads of the world need to do to succeed. Look at your department's P&T guidelines. Does it say something like "You must have two published articles before consideration will be made for tenure." Truthfully, that was something you should have looked into when you applied to Dreamjob U. And when you were interviewed, did you ask if that rule were hard and fast? Were allowances ever made? What about having two articles accepted by a major, peer-reviewing journal, but not yet published? Did you negotiate a contingency in your contract, or were you so happy just to get hired you didn't bother? **The major reason you need to publish quickly is academic survival**. The fittest are those who publish—and publish often. Whether you find yourself at a community college from which you hope to advance or an R-1 institution, publish or perish has never been truer in the academy—nor its corollary, publish and flourish.

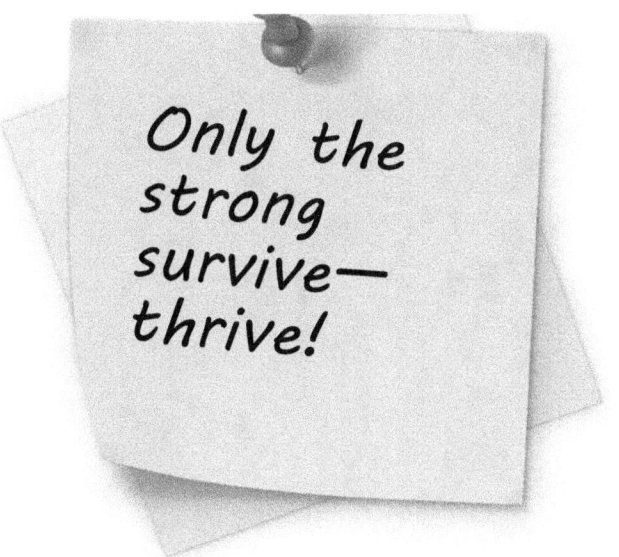

Only the strong survive— thrive!

III. DEFINING A SCHOLARLY FRAME OF MIND: ITS COMPONENTS

The Essentialness of Curiosity

When Charlie was nine, his parents sent him to summer camp, where an enterprising counselor showed him how to connect a nine-volt battery to a buzzer. Curious about the application of the demonstration, when Charlie returned home, he rigged the shut door to his room so that any time his parents or brothers tried to enter, two electrified wires touched and a buzzer sounded. The same counselor also taught him how to add an auxiliary speaker to a record player or radio. Unfortunately, Charlie plugged the wires into the wrong port of his mom's prized stereo, shooting a lightning bolt out of the speaker that blackened his ceiling. For a year he hid the spot by rubbing toothpaste across the textured ceiling so his parents wouldn't spot the damage. Bill's curiosity took a different form. He read the entire *Worldbook Encyclopedia* from A to Z while still in elementary school, which helped him develop a broad base of knowledge at an early age.

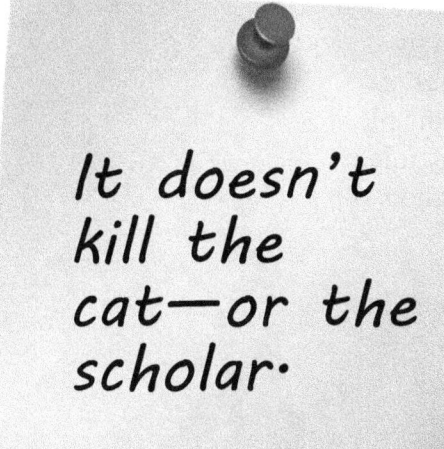

It doesn't kill the cat—or the scholar.

At a young age Charlie and Bill were obviously curious, but was that curiosity innate, stimulated by a good camp counselor, or a little of both? The question is relevant because over the years we have become more and more convinced that curiosity forms the foundation of a scholarly frame of mind. Can we teach you to be curious, stimulate you, or are we hoping you already have that trait when you read this book? Read on.

In "The Art of Fiction," Henry James describes the essential trait to would-be writers in much the same way: "Try to be one of those on whom nothing is lost," but he may just as well have been advising a scholar wanna-be. Sherwood Anderson captured the same essence when he named a story about a 15-year-old future writer "I Want To Know Why."

How curious are you and about what? Charlie never cared to know where the Nile originated or why for every action there is an equal and opposite reaction, but he recalls reading a western comic book and coming across the top-of-the-panel description "Tim dons the familiar outfit and becomes Red Mask." "Don" was always a proper noun, like his buddy Don Nelson or Don Winslow of the Navy, but how can it be used as a decapitalized verb? Eventually Charlie's Ben Franklin curiosity about electricity translated into the more literary pursuit of: how is a metaphor put together? How do the thing and the thing to which it is compared work together? Are there any "rules" about the two things being compared? It wasn't really until a graduate school course introduced him to the concept of architectonics that he got his answer. All art has structure. His entire academic career has been devoted to applying that concept to literary works in order to discover their underlying structure and then to interpret what that structure alone is saying.

Curiosity is predicated upon an open mind, a willingness to see things you don't understand as well as to consider things from others' perspectives.

Fostering a Proactive Sensibility

As a teacher-scholar, Hal created a routine his first year in teaching that stuck with him and served him well. In preparing his classes, he would constantly come across ideas he found wrong, unsupported, or something that could be better expressed. In that pre-electronic era, he developed a dual file system. If he spotted a newspaper article, a piece of research, or saw something on TV that could be used in creative writing, he jotted down a note and placed it in a file labelled FICTION. If on the other hand, in trying to stay current, he ran across something inexplicable in the literary work he was preparing, he jotted it down, often in the form of a question? As a result, the file labelled LIT CRIT bulged with sheets of paper saying things like "Why might Duke Ferrara have killed his first wife?" and "Did Margot Macomber shoot her husband accidentally, on purpose, or accidentally on purpose?"

And since he ran most of his classes through Socratic questioning, he often found himself asking questions or being asked questions by his students that he couldn't answer right away. Guess what happened to those questions? They didn't die with the end of class, but took up a new life as seeds in his greenhouse files.

If you check our *Introduction to Applied Creative Thinking* (2012), you'll find a whole chapter devoted to the notion of just recognizing these moments called IX. Basic Creative Strategies: Glimmer-Catching (pp. 41-44). Look it over in detail, and try some of the exercises at the end of the chapter.

The scholarly frame of mind is a switch that is always on.

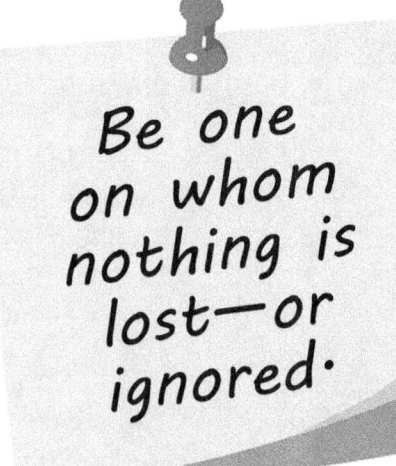

Be one on whom nothing is lost—or ignored.

Seeking Answers

If step one of a proactive sensibility is asking questions, step two is trying to answer them. To generate good questions and let those questions die on the vine without being harvested represents only half of the scholarly equation. Since Hal and Charlie shared an office for over 35 years, they spent a lot of time before and after class trying to answer these dangling questions.

One day in the FICTION file, Charlie ran across a note that said simply "Arbalest?" By then, Hal had forgotten what the notational seed meant, so they watered it through discussion. What had been merely a vocabulary word originally circled on a page and then transferred to a note was cultivated into a short story called "The Turning Point" that eventually appeared in *Mike Shayne Mystery Magazine*.

Sometimes discussion was not enough. Rough ideas like rough lumber had to be shaped into a practical product. Over the years Hal and Charlie evolved a process where they would settle upon an idea, discuss the idea until it began to takes shape, and then Charlie would go home and try to write up a single paragraph that encapsulated that idea. Sometimes, as with "The Turning Point," that meant creating the short story's opening paragraph. With lit crit, the first paragraph focuses on the thesis. For instance, Hal's question about Margot Macomber eventually led to a focus on the guide of the Macomber expedition, and a published article on Wilson, the guide, as the chief architect of the death of Hemingway Francis Macomber.

Utilizing Rigor

A scholarly mind realizes that ideas and even outlines are not enough. Likewise, curiosity and good ideas alone are insufficient. In order to address any nagging question or merely a glimmer of an idea, rigorous disciplinary protocols must be followed. Usually rigor begins with what is called a lit review or a review of the scholarship. Since ideas have been spun into a web of scholarship/research, finding out what others have said becomes paramount. The entire gamut of the scholarship/research field relevant to the point must be examined from the most current to the deep background sources. A true scholar is not interested just in what the XYZ team claims about Professor Peabody's Way-back machine, but also what Professor Peabody said and published on the subject.

Bill is a scholar and a mountain climber. He has methodically climbed all the tallest peaks in North America and loves the thrill of ascending above the tree line, which occurs on any mountain around 10,000 feet. Bill has hiked on glaciers and slept on the snow at the tops of mountains, but his climbing career began with a near death experience in the Teton's when he fell 50 feet while being belayed by a friend. Bill and his friend were neophytes at mountain climbing and were learning the elementary skills needed to ascend the highest mountains in North America. Luckily, he survived that fall and continued to struggle to the top. And so it is with scholarship. The elementary skills must be mastered before ascending to the top of the publication ladder. One must persevere to ascend above the tree line at 10,000 feet; coincidentally it takes about 10,000 hours to become great at scholarly productivity. Nevertheless, whether ascending 10,000 feet or writing for 10,000 hours, it all begins with the first few steps and mastering the elementary skills followed by a heavy dose of rigor as those skills are put into practice.

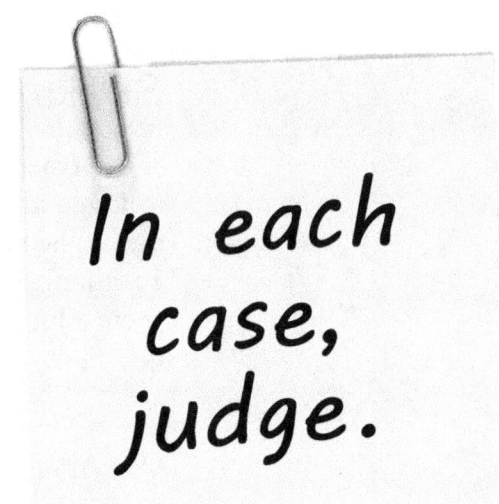

A scholarly frame of mind, then, is a critical frame of mind. Everything it scans, it scrutinizes for possible use.

Exerting Discipline

A scholarly mind is more methodical than haphazard. If a good education is, above all, a habit of mind, a good habit of that mind is being disciplined about the entire process. While certainly a good idea or even a key revision or direction to take can occur at any time or any place, discipline means not waiting for that to happen but providing a protocol that makes it happen. Such a protocol develops a regular time and place to write/research as well as the necessary equipment. Discipline also means placing weight on the various steps in the process. Charlie would rather come up with a good idea, Hal would prefer to reorganize it, Bill would opt for researching it, while nothing comes between Rusty and his trusty Apple computer. As businessman-entrepreneur Mark Cuban says, "Ideas are worthless until you do something with them" (p. 42).

While many scholars might argue that research topics simply come to you, some prefer to organize and plan methodically. Lists, notes, and folders all serve as ways of organizing information, but we often overlook the power of these same tools as idea-generation opportunities. We agree that innovative ideas come from generative thinking; however, we've also learned that the real challenge is making something meaningful of those ideas.

Rusty is usually attached to a tablet or a laptop, sometimes both at the same time. As a strategy for managing multiple major writing projects at the same time—sometimes balancing books, articles, chapters, and grants all at once—Rusty keeps detailed records using free electronic applications (apps) on his devices. Examples include Evernote and Wunderlist. Rusty manages projects closely and keeps meticulous records of their status and stage of completion. Each entry and status for an edited collection is tracked with all details, and if co-edited who did what and when, along with notes for the next round. The details managed through these technologies allow for more productive writing and fewer stalling points along the way. Rusty does not have to worry that he'll lose his place when moving from one project, manuscript, or presentation to the next. Simply put, the technology manages that aspect of the process for him, which allows for a focus on content generation, revision, and development—the bigger ideas necessary for moving the project forward.

Contributing to the Scholarly Conversation

Ultimately, **the scholarly frame of mind willingly enters into the scholarly conversation.** We all had pedants in grad courses who never minded telling us lowly grad students how they felt about a particular idea, but refused to take questions or had proudly purchased a small piece of the landscape esoterica about which nobody had any idea of its geographic features and few knew the abutting thoughts. "Art," says James in "The Art of Fiction"—although he might as well have been referencing scholarship and research—"lives upon discussion, upon experiment, upon curiosity, upon variety of attempts, upon the exchange of views and the comparison of standpoint." An idea needs to be batted and volleyed above the nets of ignorance to survive. Every new idea is willingly shared—not hoarded—in the hopes that it becomes accepted knowledge, and, obviously, what is accepted depends upon the guidelines of that particular field. The scholarly frame of mind demands risk-taking, a willingness to travel down a road even if it means discovering you have been wrong.

Guided by Excellence

While many motives dominate the scholarly frame of mind—tenure and promotion come to mind—**a true scholar is guided by the desire to excel.** Most teachers try to stay current in their disciplines, but that goal is merely a point of departure for the scholarly frame of mind. A true scholar eventually tries to carve out a niche, replacing currency with expertise. Sometimes that excellence means finding one more source or performing one more experiment or searching where none has gone before. As you would expect, the desire for excellence is very much an intrinsic trait that as we point out in *Achieving Excellence in Teaching* is difficult to cultivate.

A scholarly frame of mind rarely content with the simple answer, welcomes—indeed seeks out—complexity, scaling up and down Bloom's taxonomy like a driven mountain climber.

Conclusion

Just as would-be mountaineers must possess a determined mindset (and conditioned body) before attempting the assault, so you must cultivate what we call a scholarly frame of mind if you wish to achieve scholarly productivity. A former basketball coach at our university told us a story about an encounter with one of his players who was having trouble accepting his backup role on the team after a stellar high school career. After a lengthy discussion with the player one afternoon, Mike looked the crestfallen kid in the eye and said, "I wish I could reach in my desk, pull out a magic wand, tap your shoulder, and turn you into a star. But it's not that easy; it takes long hours and hard work."

An old Wheaties commercial used to proclaim that "Champions are made, not born." And so it is with scholars. A scholarly frame of mind comes not through the tap of a magic wand, but through the synthesis and cultivation of certain character traits. Sure, some individuals possess the needed qualities in greater abundance, but anyone with an honest desire to achieve scholarly productivity can develop these traits just as our mountain climbers can train for the climb.

Alas, the converse also remains true. If you lack these characteristics and the further ability to integrate them, the odds of your becoming a productive scholar diminish. The scholarly mind repeatedly acts to refine these traits in order to produce new knowledge and somewhere along the way—if it were not there before— develops a passion toward the process.

Never settle for pi=3.14.

References

Cuban, M. (2016, Oct.) The Cuban advantage. *Men's Fitness, 42*.

IV. TAKING INVENTORY: UNDERSTANDING WHAT IT TAKES TO SUCCEED

Having a scholarly frame of mind prepares one for the scholarly climb, but **all climbers must also take inventory of their own scholarly skills.** Assessing one's strengths and weaknesses is part of the pre-climb checklist. Would an inexperienced climber start out with the most difficult mountain face without enough rope? Two climbers in Big Bend National Park were stuck on the side of the mountain with a 600-foot descent, but each climber only had 300 feet of rope. They tied the two pieces together, but one inexperienced climber could not negotiate around the knot, was stuck in the middle of the climb, and died of hyperthermia. When you fail to prepare, you prepare to fail.

We once read that 90% of all faculty consider themselves in the top 10% of all teachers. A corollary to this rule suggests that faculty also overrate their skills in scholarship and research. Years ago Boice (1990) performed a study of scholars, determining that only 15% of the faculty at any university—regional comprehensive to R1—are practicing, continuously productive scholars. In short, 85% of newly hired faculty will not produce on a regular basis, so the odds are already stacked against most faculty succeeding.

What can you do to enhance those odds?

Mining Graduate School Experiences

1. **Scrutinize your graduate-school days for those research strategies and skills** that you evolved, both those that worked and those that didn't. Take an honest look at the capabilities you have developed.

- How good, for instance, were you at time management? Did you write all your term papers at the last possible minute? Did you actually make schedules for both writing and studying to which you stuck?

- Did you find it easy to discover a topic on which to write, or did you spend hours doodling and diverting yourself?

- Did you have trouble coming up with some sort of outline? Could you develop an hypothesis and figure out in advance what evidence you would need?

- Did your research skills hinder you? Did you know how to perform an experiment or find that key article? Were you familiar with and current on key theories in your discipline?

- Is your command of the conventions of the English language sufficient for the publishing arena? A few years ago we wrote an article for the *Journal of Faculty Development* called "The Pancaked Professor" in which we provided examples of poor grammar and organization in submitted pieces.

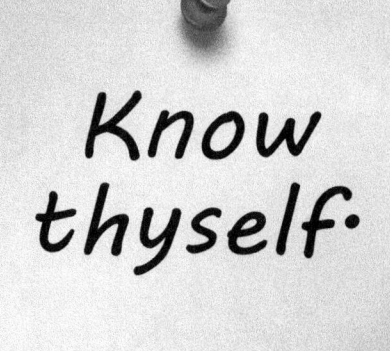

2. **Review whether you actually produced anything** in your graduate school days that is proof you can publish. Most new faculty members point to their dissertation, which is probably a good starting area. In fact, many of us have probably heard that old adage that "a solid dissertation is good for three articles or one book." Too many dissertations climb into a small niche with an even smaller audience of interested people. Many dissertations are more surveys than groundbreaking research. Some display embryonic skills, but are starting points. Some merely fulfill Ph.D. graduation requirements and sit on Mom's coffee table.

- Did you write a paper that you think provides the basis for a publishable article?

- Does your dissertation deal with an area of interest to a specific publisher? Is your dissertation not only written well enough to get you a Ph.D. but to work on the publishing higher level?

- Did a grad school prof ever suggest to you that a paper you wrote, or part of it, was a good start on a future publication?

- In your grad school research, did you ever make marginal notes of possible directions to go or even start an idea file in which you placed your "brainstorms" for future development?

3. **Examine the interpersonal systems** you favored during your graduate school days. Do they suggest any pattern you could use, or should you be working on a new pattern (e.g., networking)?

- Were you essentially a loner?

- Did you actually ask professors for suggestions during the research process from idea to draft?

- Did you ever help a grad student friend with a paper? One of Charlie's earliest publications was with a colleague from grad school. Bob became an expert in Old English, while Charlie favored American Lit, even specializing early in his career with Edgar Allan Poe. A few years out of grad school with Charlie in Kentucky and Bob in Louisiana, they collaborated on a published

article about the image of the raven, found both in Poe's poetry and Old English poetry.

- Did you participate in any group writing?

- Did you have a mentor, some professor who offered you both specific and general guidance about how to succeed in research and scholarship at graduate school and the next level?

Analyzing On-the-Job Experiences

If you are now teaching in higher ed, you can help yourself greatly by performing a mental paradigm shift. In your new job you have been taught that you now have three or four areas of focus: teaching, scholarship/research, service, and, more recently, professional development. Start considering these fields as overlapping. Specifically, don't consider your teaching assignments as a detriment to publication but as a key component thereof. 90% of what Hal and Charlie published during their earlier teaching careers came out of the classroom. Be alert for those germs of articles throughout the day. A student asks an interesting question, you have a key thought while holding an in-class discussion, or you have a discussion with a colleague at the faculty lounge or online about something that troubled you while preparing for class.

For example, Bill got the basic idea for *Achieving Excellence in Teaching* (2014) while teaching a graduate-level course in Educational Leadership on College Teaching. After lots of trial and error, he could find no appropriate text, so he came to Hal, Charlie, and Chris with a solution: "Hey, guys, let's write a book." While teaching the Introduction to Applied Creative Thinking course, Rusty not only got Hal and Charlie to help him write the text, but when he began to set up the course, he realized he needed a pre- and post-test to assess his students' learning progress. The creation of such an instrument became a published article.

Don't ignore your own backyard.

And this book came about because Bill's chair needed another course after College Teaching in order to develop a certificate program in the higher ed area.

The key is recognizing the publication opportunities that you find in your teaching environment. It's not enough to wait for them to happen, but as in Bill's and Rusty's cases, you must actually seek them out.

Service and faculty development provide similar opportunities. A few years ago as a favor to their dean, Hal and Charlie were sitting on a committee focused on regional stewardship, especially in our Appalachian service region. At first Hal and Charlie viewed the workgroup involvement as time-wasting work, but the more hours they endured on the committee, the more they saw possibilities. First of all, they suggested the group create a scholarly journal to highlight the research being done in the region. When they came up with a name for the journal, they thought their work was concluded. Oh no, said the dean, we will need some excellent articles for the first issue in order to establish its prominence. Hal and Charlie cornered Rusty, and the three of them produced an article for the first issue.

Just this week Hal, Charlie, and Rusty were mired in a committee meeting about an online faculty development resource. During a discussion on high impact practices, the focus was on the instructor when one of the committee members wondered out loud how students perceived instructional strategies, what traits they looked for in an effective teacher. Later, as Hal and Charlie were going over the notes they took on the meeting, they found that idea had actually been taken down and circled. A quick discussion followed, and they jotted down a phrase "student perceptions of effective teaching strategies." Fifteen minutes of research on the Internet convinced them they had just discovered a viable SoTL article.

As Hal and Charlie were novices in faculty development, they were forced to create a lot of forms for their CTL's programming. They soon figured out how those forms as well as their daily activities could be used as the basis for blog posts, articles, and even books. One time they were discussing with the head of institutional research how they wrote an end of the week report for their dean by listing the week's activities as they related to the unit's strategic plan. The IR guy had never heard of such a form of assessment, looked into it, found it unique, and collaborated with Charlie and Hal on an article on the format.

As a side note, being solicited to write for a journal is higher on the publication ladder than even peer-reviewed articles. Establishing yourself as an expert in the field as well as one willing and capable of producing scholarship enhances the chance of such an invitation.

V. ANALYZING THE MARKET

Perhaps it was a fellow student or even a well-meaning professor who aided you, but you walked away from graduate school with a degree and a nugget of help in your quest to be a scholar: milk your dissertation for at least three publications. While the advice isn't bad and leverages already-performed scholarship, nobody ever told you where to go next—i.e., how to get those dissertation pieces published. We have the perfect pathway up the mountain for you.

Two Roads Diverging

As in Frost's famous poem, you stand at a crossroad, and, as with Frost, the road you choose will make all the difference. If you take the right fork, you will get to your goal of tenure/publication quicker, but if you take the left fork, you may never see publication and get caught in a constant loop of submission and rejection. For us the choice is easier than it was for Frost's traveler.

The Left Fork—Write, Search, Send, and Hope

When Charlie was in grad school, he got lucky with publication. Instead of studying for a test, he wrote a humorous piece along the lines of what would have happened if a crack writer like William Shakespeare had written for TV. Mirroring his own status as a writer, Charlie placed the whole piece within the epistolary tradition of the Bard submitting program suggestions to the three big networks and their sending him back rejections with suggestions on how to modify his plays to fit their perceptions of what played well on the tube. Because Charlie had once peddled *TV Guide* door to door and read the magazine for ten years (a modicum of research), he sent the piece to them. Even though Charlie had never written for them or had a piece published before, *TV Guide* bought "The Play's the Thing" (7 June 1969) for enough money to pay Charlie's tuition for a year.

Unfortunately, this example of mostly the workings of pure chance (Charlie never sold another such humorous piece to any magazine) falsely convinced Charlie that the proper way

Get your nose out of that journal!

to publish and not perish was write it, search out a market, send it in, and hope. Occasionally that method works, but would you be willing to bet a career on that approach? Bill had a similar experience while a brand new faculty member working toward tenure. His first two articles were published, and he thought he understood how the publishing community worked, but actually he was clueless. It would be several rejections before he published again.

Consider the issue of tenure and its short window. At most universities the new professor must publish two to three articles or a book within a five-six year period. During the tenure process, the would-be scholar is closely monitored by a departmental tenure and promotion committee. Writing an article is important, submitting it is better, but it best be published—and quickly. A few years ago, the Modern language Association (MLA) came out with the finding that one in seven articles finds publication. Now if you were capable of writing one article per year—which most new scholars can't produce while attending to their other professional duties of teaching, service, professional development, and staying current in the field—statistically it would take seven years to find even one publication. And if that one publication didn't come in the first four years of the tenure process, what are the chances of your being at that university long enough to see it published?

The odds are even longer for fiction writers. When Hal and Charlie started writing mysteries in the 80s, they calculated that with the available markets and the flood of submissions, their chance of getting a story in a magazine were approximately 1 in 4000. This point was driven home to them when the first 24 mysteries they wrote and submitted were rejected by *Ellery Queen's Mystery Magazine*. Hitting the wall (which was papered with rejections slips) so many times convinced them a better way had to exist.

The Right Fork—Analyze the Market

In truth, when Charlie submitted his humorous article to *TV Guide*, he had a little more going for him than blind luck. After all, why did he select the market he did? He had also spent his youth reading *Mad* magazine and could just as easily have sent his piece to Alfred E. Neuman and the usual gang of idiots. Actually, Charlie had submitted a piece to *Mad* magazine on the writing Olympics and received a rejection slip for his troubles. However, he had always read *Mad* for the pure fun of it all, while *TV Guide* was a market he had often thought about—i.e., what kind of pieces do they publish. While he didn't have the current issues available, he had been collecting the Fall Preview issue of *TV Guide*. So he could easily read through to figure out their style (a skill he had honed from studying American and British lit in grad school). In short, he was on the cusp of the right idea, but wasn't able to fully articulate it yet.

What Charlie hadn't yet grasped at his *TV Guide* stage was the power of a business tool called **market analysis**. While writing at their booth at the local McDonald's, Hal and Charlie often engaged the owner in various discussions. In one of those Tom explained that before the parent company even let him purchase a franchise, they had performed a market analysis of various locations, checking everything from traffic patterns, to permitted sign heights, to the demographics of the city's population.

The owner's anecdote resonated with something Hal and Charlie were teaching. Early in his career, Edgar Allan Poe published a literary satire called "How to Write a Blackwood Article." This work suggests how to get published in a popular magazine of the times to which William Blackwood gave his name. Poe had read sufficient issues of *Blackwood* to ascertain certain tendencies in its pieces. In short, before the term existed, Poe had performed an early form of market analysis (not enough remains of his papers to see if he created actual charts).

Since research was another skill graduate school had inculcated in them, Hal and Charlie followed Poe's example for their target market. They read over 100 stories in a year's worth of *Ellery Queen's Mystery Magazine* (EQMM), a magazine to which they subscribed. They created a very detailed chart (a rubric before they knew that term) that listed method of narration, characters (e.g., preferred profession, types of predicaments), plot elements, (e.g., the biter bit, thriller, noir), settings, and lengths (e.g., the story, average paragraph, average sentence). They then synthesized the 100+ stories into a report on the tendencies of purchased stories. Since at that time EQMM had had only two editors from its inception, they were in essence reading the editor's mind, exploring what the editor wanted and didn't want in fiction. For instance, they discovered the mystery magazine had not published a single story in the past year containing a licensed private investigator, which helped explain about 50% of their rejections. Often a rejection comes not because of a piece's quality, but because it truly "does not meet our needs."

With EQMM simplified and synthesized, they crafted a 25th submission, and "Sudden Death" was published in the mystery magazine's acclaimed "Department of First Stories." Knowing of the existence of such a section also obviously improved their odds of publication. To capitalize on their discovery of market analysis, Hal and Charlie wrote and sold a piece to *Writer's Digest*, "On S.A.L.E.: A Technique for Breaking into the Short Story Market" (December 1982, pp. 40-43), where, cleverly, the acronym breaks down into:

- "**S**ample the market to find a particular magazine
- **A**nalyze your magazine's tendencies
- **L**ist those tendencies on a chart

- Evaluate your findings using other sources."

Not only did Hal and Charlie sell more stories, but they made more money—and garnered more publications—by also making money on marketing the process.

As an aside, we'd like to point out that statistically speaking it is more difficult to publish in popular magazines than scholarly journals (and it pays better—ever tried to cash a reprint?).

Hal and Charlie are so old that back then their promotion and tenure committee told them that even though they were teaching creative writing, publishing poetry and fiction didn't help their vita's record of publications. With that prohibition in mind and since market analysis had worked so well with for fiction, they decided to modify market analysis for publishing literary criticism.

As with the Shakespeare article, Charlie had enjoyed only moderate success with literary publication. While teaching Edwin Arlington Robinson's poetry in his Intro to Am Lit class, Charlie came up with a unique interpretation. The first place he sent "A Re-examination of 'Richard Cory'" was the *Colby Library Quarterly* (CLQ) and they published it (9.11, September 1972, pp. 579-582). Prior to submission, Charlie had never heard of the journal, but, knowing Robinson was from Maine, he looked up journals published in the pine tree state. On the inside cover of one of those journals, CLQ, he found the editor's statement "This Quarterly is primarily interested in Maine authors . . . ." So Charlie, having done some simple market analysis that was not as thorough as that for EQMM, was more than lucky when his article found a home.

One of the first journals Hal and Charlie analyzed was *Studies in Short Fiction* (SSF). They both taught courses with short stories in them, and Charlie had been subscribing to the journal since grad school, so his office held almost eight years of SSF on the shelves. This time Hal and Charlie created a card file with an index card for each article published. Eventually they were able to synthesize the cards into what a typical SSF article looked like in terms of length, critical approach, and even favored authors. Charlie had also accumulated some rejection slips that went beyond the usual "This does not suit our needs" to helpful comments that were just a step below "Revise and resubmit." Over the years they published more than a dozen pieces in that journal, and when an associate editor moved to a new journal in Washington, DC, they sent her some pieces.

Other Types of Market Analysis

Early in their careers **Hal and Charlie also discovered that market analysis was not a purely academic process.** Coming across a quote supposedly from Robert Frost that "It's hard to hate someone up close," they decided to put it to the test. They set out to make **personal contact** with editors, often finding them at conventions presenting panels and sitting in the hallway. With their short stories, they often solicited help from such people as Mike Nevins (film and Ellery Queen scholar), who read over a story of theirs in a bar and critiqued it on the spot, John Updike and Alison Lurie, who offered encouragement and specific advice, and the most helpful of all, John D. MacDonald, who explained his own writing habits in great deal at a convention in his name. A local writer offered his agent to them. Another agent was found because they knew her husband, a sci fi writer of renown.

Once they were at a convention in Nashville when they looked out their hotel room to see the building across from them housed several different magazines that accepted fiction. On a lark they walked over, found everyone was out to lunch but one person, and began to talk with him. He turned out to be the editor of one of the magazines, and before they left, Hal and Charlie had secured his card and his promise to read any submission to his magazine personally. Over the years that personal connection resulted in a lot of sales to that magazine.

Throughout their publishing careers, Hal and Charlie carried on **active correspondences** with various editors. After accepting their "Sudden Death," editor Fred Dannay, the then-living half of the Ellery Queen writing team, understood how hard it was for co-written stories to be accepted, so Fred gave them their long-standing pen-name of Hal Charles. Trying to break into *Mike Shayne Mystery Magazine*, Hal and Charlie were thwarted not by the editor but by the assistant editor named Chuck Fritch. Even though Chuck was rejecting their stories, he sent them helpful advice, eventually signing the rejection slips so they learned his identity. When the magazine's editor suddenly died, Chuck took over as editor, and, owing to their longtime familiarity with the man and his editorial standards, Hal and Charlie sold him a lot of mystery and detective fiction.

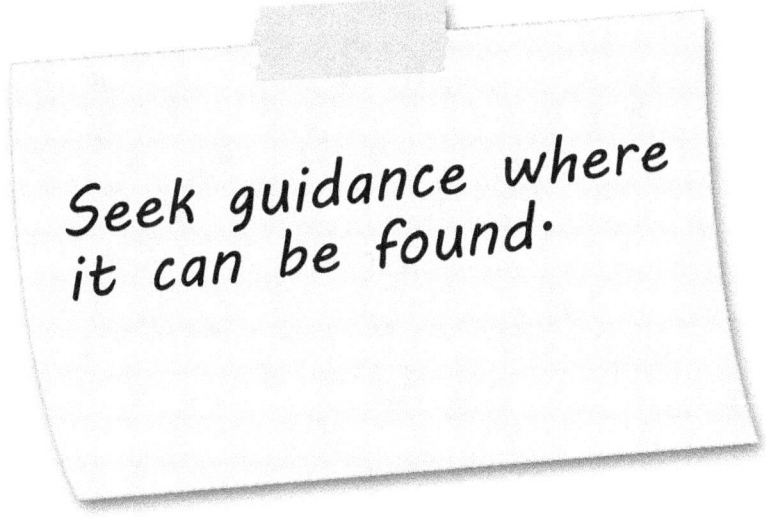

Seek guidance where it can be found.

Over a decade ago Hal and Charlie attended the Lilly Conference and sat down at a table in the registration center to drink coffee and eat a banana. Someone asked if a chair was free, they said yes, a conversation ensued, and the man turned out to be the editor of a prominent teaching and learning journal. Hal and Charlie have had Gregg come down to our university to speak about what editors want and even have co-written an article with him.

Supporting Sources for Analysis

In the S.A.L.E. article, we emphasized that evaluation could be accomplished "using other sources." What did we mean? Before the Internet, if you sent an S.A.S.E. to a publication, you could get them to send you a tip sheet. Now, if you search the Internet, you'll find magazines and journals have their own websites with available tips. It has become commonplace for all new editors to write a Preface in the first issue of a journal they take over in which they explain for what they are looking. Some editors publish tips for their publication in other journals as *Minnesota Review* editor Jeffrey Williams did in the *Chronicle of Higher Education*. New Forums, for instance, has a website for which we write a weekly blog that includes, among other things, hints on academic and creative writing.

And don't forget personal contact. Perhaps that person in the office next to you has just gone through a rigorous revise and resubmit procedure for a prestigious journal. Go to lunch or have coffee with him/her. Email colleagues from grad school or places you have taught for help. Academia can be one big support community.

Indeed, **effective market analysis takes many forms.** Regardless of whether your analysis results from a personal contact with the editor or a detailed profile evolved from extensive reading and research, however, taking this fork in the road not only gives you more focus for your critical piece, but also greatly improves your chances of publication.

VI. BECOMING A DISCIPLINED SCHOLAR USING SOARS GUIDELINES

One day in the Chihuahuan Desert Bill passed a motorist on the side of the road at the foot of a mountain flailing his arms in distress. He was out of water, out of food, and his car battery was dead. He was exhausted, bruised, and cut. The story slowly emerged that the day before he had seen this great mountain rising eight thousand feet out of the desert floor, became infatuated with it, left his car, with the lights on, and summited the mountain without using a map or a trail. He got to the top and viewed an incredible sunset. Because he had no flashlight for the return trip, he slept on the ground without a sleeping bag, food, or water and stumbled back down to his car the next morning. This hiker is like the scholar who becomes enamored with writing and rushes up the publication mountain without discipline and focus for the assent. The results for both the mountain climber and the scholar can be catastrophic.

Becoming a scholar is like following a well-worn path to the summit, learning from those who have walked the path before, following a path that is methodical and well traveled. Scholars continuously seek knowledge in a methodical way—they absorb it, analyze it, and then disseminate it. In order to share what they have learned, the most effective scholars follow the same basic trail to publication that includes the following steps: **S**et up, **O**rganize, **A**rgue, **R**eview and Revise, then **S**ubmit (**SOARS**).

Follow the leaders.

Set Up

First, begin your journey by setting goals for writing; remember, a writer is one who writes. To be better prepared for hiking up mountains, Bill has determined to run three days a week for forty minutes on a treadmill. He has a specific goal of what he is going to do, where he is going to do it, and when. He does the same thing with writing. Three days a week he writes for an hour in a secluded place far away from distractions. To be successful as a scholar, you should determine what to write, where to write, when to write, and a production goal.

- **Decide what to write**. Catch glimpses of an idea, write it down, and begin research. Many ideas come while teaching, reading, and during scholarly conversations. The university and professional conferences are great times to join in discussions with other scholars about important issues in the field. Jot down any ideas that come out of these discussions and begin researching the relevant literature. Keep all scholarly ideas in a file (either hard copy or electronic), and come back to them for inspiration as needed. At a recent Pedagogicon between sessions we began speaking to a counterpart at another state regional university about the problems of classroom observation, which sparked an idea. Six months later we're collabo-writing an article.

- **Find a place to write**. Bill started out writing in his office at the University and found that it was impossible to concentrate with a plethora of interruptions. Is there a nook in the library to get away from students and colleagues? Is there a place at home? Is there a place in the community that is ideal? Increase the possibility of success by finding that place and going there as a regular habit. Establishing a place provides a space between stimulus and response; in that space your juices can flow freely. Rusty writes early every morning at the breakfast table with his Fruit Loops and laptop in front of him. Hal prefers an upstairs, semi-darkened room and a retro yellow tablet. Charlie composes on his trusty desktop computer both at the office and at home.

- **Set a time to write everyday**. To be terrific, be specific; pick a time when productivity is highest and make this time a priority, even setting the hours aside as sacred. This discipline may be one of the most difficult to develop because so many important tasks need to be accomplished in so little time. Classes have to be taught, meetings need to be attended, and students are not interruptions but the very reason for our existence. Yet, if time is not carved out for scholarly productivity, then other things will fill the vacuum. Studies show that most people are productive during the middle of the day. Hal, Charlie, and Bill fit into this category. On the other hand, 10% are morning doves (Rusty), and 10% are night owls (all of us in grad school).

- **Focus on a production goal**. While some seasoned scholars set a goal to write 1,000-2,000 words a day, you may be more comfortable with 500 in the beginning. Regardless of the specific word count, your goal is possible only when time is set-aside at a place suitable for reflection and writing. During this time you must focus on your task (interestingly, none of us can write with music in the background). Remember that activity is not productivity, particularly if emails and social media take the place of scholarly writing. Our production goals vary, usually according to the task. For instance, every Monday Charlie writes a 750-1000-word blog. Hal writes a novel chapter of about 1000 words every other day. Rusty works on so many different types of writing that he has to keep a chart, but that's another chapter.

Organize

Once you have determined a time, place, and word count, you can focus on the production process. A scholar should not just have one idea but a basket full of ideas; that is, you should have several pieces in various stages of completion. For each piece, the actual production process involves reading widely, taking notes and making a detailed outline. **Essentially, you are a cook preparing different dishes—one on the chopping board being prepared, one simmering on the back burner, and one boiling on the front burner.**

- **Read widely**. Once the idea for a piece begins to heat up, it is important to read widely to learn what others have to say about the topic. Start with the most recent scholarship on the topic. This action not only provides you with the latest views on the subject, but if the writer is thorough, the article/chapter will offer you a timeline of previous relevant scholarship. Be particularly aware of those views which support or dispute your germinal idea. When Hal and Charlie were teaching Browning's "My Last Duchess," they began to research why Duke Ferrara might have killed his last duchess. The more literary criticism they read on the Duke's motivation (and critics had been discussing that problem for over a century), the more they became convinced that critics were overlooking the imagery of sterility in the Duke's own words. Sometimes the best ideas and theses come from reading and not finding what you're looking for.

- **Mark your sources**. What you are looking for are key points in an article. Always highlight the source's thesis. Find the arguments that support the thesis. Examine the data used to undergird the argument's claims. You can supplement your findings through conversations with trusted colleagues, especially if they have expertise in the field. For instance, when Hal and Charlie got their insight on Browning, they went next door to a long-time colleague, a Victorian Era expert, who heard their brilliant theory—and laughed. A day later Mike came by their office and confessed the idea actually held merit and pointed them toward a secondary source with which they were not familiar. Had he not laughed, they would have added Mike's name to the credits when the piece was published in *Studies in Browning and His Circle*.

- **Evaluate the findings**. Synthesize the ideas gleaned from your reading, reflections, and conversations. At this point you should be starting to come up with a thesis, or if you had a proposed thesis going into the research, you should be refining it. Hal and Charlie hard copy every piece of research and write copious marginal notations. Rusty prefers Track Changes in Word. Excerpt the most salient points for easy recall as you start putting the piece together. Hal and Charlie use yellow markers, while Rusty prefers different colors. When Hal and Charlie finish an article, they always write a comment on the top of the first page that rates an article (excellent, useless, great lit review) as well as lists it usable fundamental and powerful concepts. Sometimes at the top of researched articles they all write a temporary thesis to be the basis for their article.

- **Make a preliminary outline**. Once you have the embryo of a thesis (whether you started with it or developed it along the way), start with a rough list of the main topics that need to be discussed. As the writing progresses, revisit the outline and make needed changes. Be sure that your ideas mesh smoothly and lend themselves to support from your sources. In the case of this book, for instance, after research we produced a temporary outline just to get us started. However, because of our weekly meetings, conversations, and detailed review of what we were writing, the outline changed on a weekly basis. As Mike Tyson once said about a fight, "Everybody has a plan until you hit 'em in the mouth."

Take a hint from Julia Child and don the chef's toque.

Argue

From the outline you move to a first draft. **The key to every article is its argument, and the essence of the argument is contained in its thesis.** At this point your preliminary thesis gets sharpened. You might start not with the actual article, but creating an abstract for the article, which is nothing more than your outline in narrative prose (vs. the fragmentary notes that dominate outlines) wherein you hit the most fundamental and powerful concepts, is an alternate way to go. The argument, then, contains the thesis and the rationale for the article, all stated within 100-150 words, depending upon the publication.

- **What matters most?** The abstract should focus attention on what matters most and become the spine of the argument. For example, this book's argument is that every professor can achieve scholarly productivity by following our suggested strategies. Every section, every sentence, and every word must contribute to the thesis.

- **Organization.** Organize your article around your argument, set writing goals, and timelines, and then write something everyday. For example, the authors of this book started with an argument about the importance of scholarship and the specific strategies to follow to accomplish that goal. Once they had a thesis, they created a rough outline/Table of Contents that changed every time they wrote a chapter. Each member of the group tried to write 500 words per day on this article (though, truthfully, they were also writing other pieces the same day).

Review and Revise

Create an effective writing methodology. **Begin every writing session by reading over previous work and revising.** All that is written needs to be reviewed by colleagues and revised; write then rewrite. A good friend has published hundreds of books and articles. Bill asked him one day, "Do you need to revise your writing, or because of practice is the first draft worthy of publication?" Surprisingly he responded, "I rewrite a dozen times before I am satisfied with my words." Hemingway revised the end of one of his novels twenty-nine times.

What you can't see is the discipline underlying the organization for this book. Usually, one person was assigned a chapter or part of a chapter, which was due one week after the assignment at the next regular meeting of the group. Almost always that chapter or part of a long/complex chapter was sent out before the meeting or provided at the meeting. Every chapter was revised by another writer. Some chapters needed five or six revisions. It's not easy sometimes seeing what you thoughts were perfectly crafted sentences ripped out and replaced with something new. However, all of us subscribed to the old Hollywood axiom that "Nothing is written—everything is rewritten."

- **Seek Criticism**. Since not everyone collabo-writes like we do, have colleagues or friends read and critique all writing. We review each other's work weekly in our writing group. Ask colleagues to look at your writing from a macro and then a micro level. Truthfully, sometimes you have to micro edit first so that the copy reads smoothly enough for you to focus on the macro level.

- **Macro edit.** Is the overall writing significant, organized in a meaningful manner, does it make sense, and is it a good argument? During a recent weekly conversation the authors met to revise an outline for a book that was halfway finished. Through a scholarly discussion, they decided to make three major revisions that significantly changed the scope of the book. This course correction happens more often than one might think because as you write, you learn, or as the poet Theodore Roethke says, "I learn by going where I have to go."

- **Micro edit.** Draw on the strength of a great editor and a wordsmith. Have an editor look hard at word selection, grammar, punctuation, and paragraph form. One of the authors of this book, Hal, is our designated editor. He reviews every word, every sentence, and every paragraph to ensure we use the English language to our advantage, not our disadvantage. Three of the four of us are professors of English who have been editing our entire careers. As such, we have learned of the two great curses of production, perfection and rejection.

- **Realize you can only approach perfection, not attain it**. Some writers wait on perfection before they want to submit their work; therefore, the work never gets out the door. Once Lincoln was seen running down Pennsylvania Avenue chasing after key words stored in his top hat while preparing for a speech. He was rearranging the words over and over to make greatest impact. He worked to perfect the words and the sentences into one of the greatest speeches of all time delivered on a battlefield in a little Pennsylvania town called Gettysburg. It would be a shame if Lincoln never gave the speech but just kept perfecting his sentences and key words. At some time, you, like Lincoln, are going to have to deliver your speech (to a publisher). Anne Bradstreet likened the process to kicking your children out of the nest. They may not be fully formed or ready for the world, but at some point they have to try on their own.

- **Fear not rejection—rather, learn from it.** Other writers are devastated by rejection and are frozen in the process. Accept criticism and rejection as part of the learning process of how to publish. If MLA has found you will have to submit seven times to gain an acceptance, don't worry about the other six. Think of them the way Edison treated failure—now you have learned 999 ways not to write your article. See our chapter on market analysis, and study reviews of your writing and improve the text. Review and revise the piece and send it out the door.

Submit

Submit each work to only one publisher at a time, but work on several projects concomitantly. The authors of this book have so many writing projects going on at the same time that they have to be very organized to keep track of each piece. They will not wait on the completion of one project before launching into the next one. Currently, they are working on a novel, a textbook, a book in the New Forums Series, "It Works for Me," a weekly blog post, and other ideas at various stages. When one publication is sent to the publisher, others are in the process of being completed. There is no wait time; they write something everyday, revise something else, write and rewrite, think and ponder, and read widely to gain new insights and ideas. They sometimes publish with little revision, but they also have worked on one article for three years that was revised several times. To complete a groundbreaking article on creative pedagogy, Hal and Charlie took seven years (obviously they had tenure at the time).

Each time they submitted their work to only one publisher at a time and waited for a response, but they worked on other projects while they waited. This process is very important for two reasons. First, publishers will blackball an author who submits an article to more than one publication at a time. Imagine the consequences if one submitted an article to several publishers and all of them accepted the piece. Secondly, psychologically it is im-

You must establish a clear and focused direction.

perative that writing becomes a continuous process uninterrupted by rejection and disappointment. If one writes and waits, the waiting can become a time to develop writers block.

Here are some other suggestions for submission.

- **Keep an inventory** of everything that is in preparation, boiling, and simmering on the back burner. It is easy to forget where publications have been submitted, when they were submitted, and where to go next, especially after you begin placing your efforts. Set up an Excel spreadsheet or download an app to keep an inventory of works in progress. When rejections come, read the reviews, revise, record, and send the new work back out immediately.

- **Use the staircase approach to submitting**. Rather than leaping up to the first floor of writing a book or article for publication, use a set of steps. Begin with a scholarly conversation with peers, capture thoughts by writing an opinion or a brief note, and then compose an abstract for a conference presentation. Or, start at the basement of the staircase by presenting your thoughts in your class; if that goes well do some additional research and submit to a state conference. And if you get that conference gig, always end a presentation early and invite questions or comments. Gather thoughts, criticism, and research and then submit a proposal to a national or international audience. Seek input from the session attendees and revise the paper being developed. Once your argument has been vetted by some of these groups, then it is likely ready to be submitted for publication. Charlie and Hal used to regale each other on Mondays with grammatical errors they heard sportscasters make over the weekend. On a lark, they submitted a proposal for a series of negative awards a la ESPN's ESPYs to a regional pop culture convention. It was accepted as the keynote speech. After the presentation, Hal and Charlie had friends sending them verbal bloopers. Eventually, Hal and Charlie wrote the piece up, started to send it to a pop culture journal, sent it instead to a newspaper chain, and received a huge paycheck for what had once been a mere source of Monday morning amusement.

Some Guidelines

The following **SOARS guidelines will** help you scale the scholarly productivity mountain by following a well-worn path:

- **S**etup to write regularly;

- **O**rganize your scholarly work by following the protocol in one publication;

- **A**rgue a point of interest in a half-page abstract;

- **R**eview with colleagues and revise based on comments;
- **S**ubmit, especially by using the staircase approach to publication.

VII. UTILIZING BOYER'S UNDERSTANDING OF SCHOLARLY MOUNTAINS

When at that magnificent moment in "The Sound of Music" that Julie Andrews exhorts the von Trapp children to "Climb Every Mountain," she fails to advise them that each mountain is different. Scaling Mount Everest takes a great deal more skill than climbing Pilot Knob in your backyard.

Just as different size mountains exist, so it is with scholarship. In 1990 Ernest Boyer published *Scholarship Reconsidered* that created the definitive classification scheme for scholarship. In our *It Works for Me as a Scholar-Teacher* (2008), we cite Boyer's table wherein he points out that in 1969 21% of "All Respondents" (i.e., at all universities from two-year to research types) said they "Strongly Agree" with the statement, "In My Department It Is Difficult for a Person to Achieve Tenure If He or She Does Not Publish." By 1989 that percentage had grown to 42% (p. 12). We would argue that while we have no comparable studies for 2017, that percentage is close to 100%.

Boyer provides an excellent rationale for our preference for the term "scholarship" over "research." Scholarship predates the word research, which "was first used in England in the 1870s by reformers who wished to make Cambridge and Oxford 'not only a place of teaching, but of learning.'" Scholarship, Boyer continues, "in earlier times referred to a variety of creative work carried on in a variety of places, and its integrity was measured by the ability to think, communicate, and learn" (p. 15).

Boyer also clarifies the reason for his famous book. After citing a higher education study of more than eight hundred administrators that confirmed "it would be a good idea to view scholarship as more than research," Boyer believed "a broader, more capacious meaning" (p. 16) was needed to describe what it is that scholars actually do.

The message is clear: **at most institutions you must publish to achieve tenure**, and even at those two-year schools where publication is not necessary for tenure, **publication is the shibboleth for advancement.** Understanding Boyer's schema is an essential skill for scaling as well as understanding why scholars climb every mountain.

The Scholarship of Discovery

The scholarship of discovery, the first Boyer category, is often used as a synonym of research. This type focuses on an endeavor that "contributes not only to the stock of human knowledge, but also to the intellectual climate of a college or university" (p. 17). It is born of a desire to know, and it represents a new idea or product or system. The field of discovery varies from linguistics to chemistry, astronomy to anthropology, and politics to genetics. Sometimes it produces new medicines and sometimes Gatorade.

The Scholarship of Integration

The scholarship of integration is often trans-disciplinary, crossing between two or more fields and sometimes within a field by relating two apparent dissimilarities. According to Boyer, it's "making connections across the disciplines, placing specialties in a larger context, illuminating data in a revealing away," resulting in "a disciplined work that seeks to interpret, draw together, and bring new insight to bear on original research" (pp. 18-19). Yes, this form is related to the previous type: it seeks meaning more than pure knowledge.

The Scholarship of Application

The scholarship of application reflects the belief that higher education is not an island, but a part of a larger community. Here the scholar determines a social use. Sometimes, as Boyer says, "New intellectual applications can arise out of the very act of application—whether in medical diagnosis, serving clients in psychotherapy, shaping public policy, creating an architectural design, or working with the public schools" (p. 23). The ivory tower and Trump Tower exist side by side so that we have no Tower of Babel.

The Scholarship of Teaching [and Learning]

The Scholarship of Teaching and Learning, or SoTL, as it is often called today, has evolved past Boyer's original weak definition. Starting with the notion that "good teaching often means that faculty, as scholars, are also learners," Boyer concludes, "teaching, at its best, means not only transmitting knowledge but transforming and extending it as well. Through reading, through classroom discussion, and surely through questions and comments posed by students, professors

Use the coin of the realm—the toll booth won't accept Euros.

themselves will be pushed in creative new directions" (p. 24). Is this form published research, Boyer never answers, but scholars in the past 25 years, especially Maryellen Weimer in *Enhancing Scholarly Work on Teaching & Learning* (2006), have broadened the spectrum to include publications from educational research to what she calls "practitioner pedagogical scholarship" (p. 21). In his survey Boyer discovered that when asked "Do your interests lie primarily in research or in teaching," 70% responded the latter and 30% the former (p. 44). SoTL suggests that you become a teacher-scholar, integrating your interests.

The Scholarship Creative Endeavor

Scholarship is not always critical in nature.

The scholarship of creative endeavor, if you are ever asked, cannot be found in Boyer's original quartet, but is now recognized at most institutions of higher learning, most often in the arts and humanities. After his quartet, Boyer urged that "faculty assessment take into account a broader range of writing" and as an example he lists popular writing, which "should be recognized as a legitimate scholarly endeavor" (p. 35). **Dramatic performances, renderings in mediums from oil to clay to marble, and published poems, plays, and novels/short stories are all examples of creative endeavors.** A chart demonstrating that the height of creative powers for a poet is about age 30, while a novelist peaks 15 years later provides evidence that Boyer recognized the importance of creative efforts. Likewise, when Anderson and Krathwohl presented their revision of Bloom's Taxonomy, **creating** assumed the pinnacle position on the pyramid.

We are constantly amazed at scholars who refuse to believe that creative endeavors demand research. In *Borrowing Brilliance* (2009) David Kord Murray claims that the essence of creativity is borrowing, "Using an existing idea as the material to construct a new idea" (p. 61). To create the artist must borrow, and borrowing demands research, whether it's mining personal experience, studying the technique of a predecessor, or literally looking something up. Charlie and Hal once published a story called "The Death of Charety" set in 1640. Obviously, they knew little about New England in that time and had to find various sources, borrow from them, and standing on the shoulders of Nathaniel Hawthorne and Caleb Snow recreate their own fiction.

The Frontiers of Scholarship

The concept of scholarship is fluid. We have already noted how in 1990 Boyer had not quite progressed to SOTL or the scholarship of creative endeavor, but he did stress that the scholar worked in the frontiers of knowledge. We expect the academy will keep on expanding these areas and redefining those that currently exist. Consider, for instance, that when Boyer published *Scholarship Reconsidered*, the Internet did not yet exist as we know it. Those of us who wrote our doctoral dissertations on typewriters are amazed what the computer allows, but is high tech just a tool or perhaps a new field in itself? In our way of thinking, the scholarship of technology is one or two scholars away from fruition.

As we explained in *It Works for Me as a Scholar-Teacher* (2008), Judy, a colleague of ours, has written extensively in what she calls the scholarship of service, which is not quite Boyer's scholarship of application. We write weekly post for a New Forums blog called "Welcome Scholars," and in print we have called blogging "scholarship lite." Is a post just a lightweight example of any of Boyer's types, or is it an embryo that deserves its own field?

Years ago Hal and Charlie were selling mystery short stories to *Ellery Queen's Mystery Magazine* (EQMM) and *Mike Shayne Mystery Magazine*(MSMM), while at the same time they were publishing peer-reviewed literary criticism in popular journals in their field of English. Some days they would be working at the beginning of their writing session on the latest ghost-written novella (about 20,000 words) as the lead story in MSMM and finishing the session by writing about Edgar Allan Poe for *Studies in Short Fiction*. This Jeckyll-Hyde existence caused them more than once to consider combining the two apparently dissimilar types of scholarship. 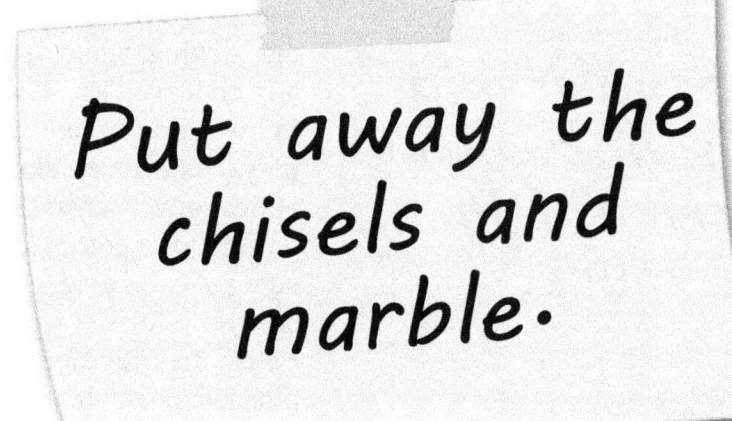 Knowing that Poe had composed a trio of short stories about C. Auguste Dupin that are credited with starting detective fiction, and that Poe also wrote the enigmatic "The Fall of the House of Usher," they began a great what-if experiment. What if Poe had sent his own detective Dupin to discover why the House of Usher fell? The result was published in *Clues*, a literary journal that published mystery and detective criticism but agreed to publish their story.

In which scholarship category does their tale fit? Is it the obvious scholarship of creative endeavor, or perhaps it fits in Boyer's scholarship of discovery, the usual category for lit crit? Or maybe it exemplifies the scholarship of integration as it combines two categories? To this day, Hal and Charlie call it **fictional criticism**, a new category of scholarship.

References

Anderson, L. & Krathwohl, D. (2001). *A taxonomy for learning, teaching, and assessing: A revision of Bloom's taxonomy*. New York: Longman.

Blythe, H. & Sweet, C. (2008). *It works for me as a scholar-teacher: Shared tips for the classroom*. Stillwater: New Forums.

Boyer, E. (1990). *Scholarship reconsidered: Priorities of the professoriate*. San Francisco: Jossey-Bass.

Murray, D. (2009). *Borrowing brilliance*. New York: Gotham Books.

VIII. THE IMPORTANCE OF SoTL

The previous chapter provided a condensed description of Boyer's categories of scholarship by way of an introduction to possible approaches you might take, the optional paths to the scholarship summit. Obviously, your discipline will strongly influence the path you take: the natural sciences and the humanities might favor the Scholarship of Discovery and Integration (with a segment of the humanities branching off into the Scholarship of Creative Endeavor), while the social sciences and such professional areas as law and business might lean toward the Scholarship of Application. Of course, these preferences are not 100%, but they do often factor into directions that tenure and evaluation committees point their candidates.

One of Boyer's categories (if we understand the extended and updated definition we used in the previous chapter), however, lends itself to any of the disciplines, the Scholarship of Teaching and Learning (SoTL). In order to understand fully the scope and potential importance of this type of scholarly endeavor, one must view it in the context of teaching itself.

The Three Stages of Teaching

A few years ago we wrote a book about phase one in climbing another mountain important to professorial success: that of teaching taxonomy. In *Achieving Excellence in Teaching* (2014) we detailed the characteristics of the **excellent teacher**. While others define the term by such things as student surveys, peer observation, and teaching portfolios, we created an assessment tool called R.A.T.E. whereby teachers, their colleagues, and their students could all evaluate teaching.

Scholarly teaching involves a process.

The next stage up the mountain is usually called **scholarly teaching**. To characterize this class, Hutchings and Shulman (1999) add to the excellent teacher "certain practices of classroom assessment and evidence gathering, when it is informed not only by the latest ideas in the field but by current ideas about teaching the field, when it invites peer collaboration and review" (p. 13). McKinney (2004) claims, "scholarly teachers do things such as reflect on their teaching, use classroom assessment techniques, discuss teaching issues with colleagues, try new things. And read and apply the literature on teaching and learning in their discipline and, perhaps, more generally." **Scholarly teaching, then, begins with**

metacognition or reflection, begets an experiment in teaching, and follows up that experiment with some sort of assessment.

The third stage of the mountain was described back in in 1999 by Hutchings and Shulman as the **scholarship of teaching** as they tried to do what Boyer hadn't almost a decade earlier, "draw a sharp line between excellent teaching and the scholarship of teaching" (p. 13). For what is now known as the scholarship of teaching and learning, they added four characteristics to scholarly teaching: "being public ('community property'), open to critique and evaluation, and in a form that others can build on . . . [and] question-asking, inquiry and investigation, particularly around issues of student learning" (p. 13). The Carnegie Foundation (2001) uses this definition for SoTL: "problem posing about an issue of teaching and learning, study of the problem through methods appropriate to the disciplinary epistemologies, applications of result to practice, communication of results, self-reflection, and peer review." We define SoTL simply as **published reflection/ research on teaching and student learning**.

Our Rationale for Performing SoTL

Perhaps one of the greatest recent recognitions by the academy is that **good scholarship and effective teaching need not be mutually exclusive**, even at both extremes of the higher education continuum (R1s and community colleges). As a result, a new ideal has emerged, the **scholar teacher**, a concept often reflected in the phrase scholarly teaching. While Maryellen Weimer claims in *Enhancing Scholarly Work on Teaching & Learning* (2006) that "There is no relationship between research and teaching" (p. 169), she does confirm on the very next page that "Doing pedagogical research does make you a better teacher" (p. 170). Nelson (2016) argues, "Excellent teaching often occurs in the absence of SoTL. However, teaching is more likely to be excellent if informed by SoTL." In short, the scholarship of teaching and learning daily grows in importance.

SoTL's growing popularity provides a host of publication opportunities. In a recent blog, Weimer (2015) calculates "there are close to 100 pedagogical periodicals." That amount is greater than the publishing opportunities available in many disciplines.

As SoTL is still in its infancy, it needs a body of scholarship to authenticate it with the academy. Each insight, each reflection, and each research study on pedagogy and student learning you conduct makes SoTL more acceptable. As we have noted elsewhere, we have contributed to popular culture, creativity studies, and even faculty development in order to bring more acceptability to the process.

SoTL offers a great opportunity for application by adapting general studies to particular disciplines and specific disciplinary research to the field as a whole. Whichever direction you go here, you are helping both your field and the entire area of the scholarship of teaching and learning.

If you look at the traditional responsibilities of teaching and research, picture them not as separate circles but as part of a Venn diagram (for that matter, you can also picture service as part of the Venn diagram). SoTL lies in the fertile ground of overlapping Venn diagrams and thus provides help for each.

SoTL exists on a large continuum from practitioner written reflection to pure educational research. Somewhere along this continuum you can find a place to join in. If you wish, you can start by writing a daily/weekly reflection on your insights into teaching. At the opposite end of the spectrum you can go to our chapter on the pattern of educational research.

SoTl provides a process for figuring out your curiosity as you go. Friberg (2016) believes, "Faculty engage in SoTL to generate/study innovations in teaching, apply and study innovative pedagogies, and better understand the complexities of teaching and learning" (Miller-Young 2015). Years ago, for instance, Hal and Charlie started team-teaching. They both prepared the course's syllabus and both showed up every class period to teach. They thought all team-teachers did the same thing until one day they participated in a panel on team-teaching wherein a group of honors professors discussed how they team-taught with each instructor facilitating class about half the time. In short, they saw team teaching as a relay race where the baton was handed off about once a week. That presentation provoked Hal and Charlie to do some research on collaborative teaching that they published in *The Teaching Professor* as "Total Team Teaching—Sharing Teaching Duties Equally" (2004). Over the years since then, they have published extensively on collaborative teaching and collabo-writing.

SoTl provides a simple staircase for one to progress as a scholar teacher. In our *Achieving Excellence in Teaching* (2014), we describe the five-stages of the scholarly mind:

1. Stage I: The Anti-Scholar

2. Stage II: The Indifferent Lurker

3. Stage III: The Interested Aficionado

4. Stage IV: The Active Scholar

5. Stage V: The Powerhouse Professional

Basically, our growing number of publications on collaboration as we ascended the staircase offers an example of the successful climb.

Characteristics of an Effective Piece of SoTL

One, **SoTL has as its ultimate goal the enhancement of student learning.** No matter how brilliant a teaching insight might be, one needs to be able to demonstrate student learning improves because of it. The mere introduction of a new piece of technology into your class, for example, might be fun or provide variety, but neither point means students are learning more.

Two, **SoTL is usually innovative, though it may also exist to support an old "truism."** For instance, we have become strong advocates of an old form made new, the mini-lecture. Occasionally spending 10-12 minutes on primarily lecturing about a topic can still promote student learning without falling back on the old staple of the full-class lecture devoid of active learning. Hal and Charlie's article on "Keeping It C.R.I.S.P." (2008) achieved innovation mainly through synthesis. We summed up some major principles of good classroom organization by creating a simple acronym.

Three, **SoTL offers systematic evidence of support for your new student learning gem.** Sometimes you utilize others' research, and other times you conduct original research. For our theory of the mini-lecture we did both, citing John Medina's *Brain Rules* (2008) and conducting our own student surveys. Bill uses the mini-lecture in all of his online classes by taping the key concepts of a lecture, always limiting his remarks to about ten minutes. This section is followed up by a reading assignment and a reflection writing assignment.

Four, **SoTL often brings to bear research not from one's field but other disciplines.** While we are faculty developers and literary critics, John Medina is a noted neuroscientist, and for us to read his material sometimes means looking up the meaning of one word per sentence. As an aside, the more you do SoTL, the more you become fascinated with trans-disciplinary knowledge; in fact, you find yourself reading in all sorts of areas where you have no formal training. Charlie, for instance, now subscribes to the *Wall Street Journal* because he found so many business insights were applicable to faculty development, and he can check his stocks on a daily basis.

For teaching's yin, scholarship provides a yang.

Five, **SoTL teaches the practitioner how to engage in a scholarly conversation.** Note in our definition of SoTL your work must be published. Publication invites others to participate in a dialogue. When you go public, you usually find the weaknesses in your theory. First, you have to get your submission by two to three journal readers plus the editor. As editor of the *Journal of Faculty Development*, Rusty has been known to work with some would-be writers through up to a dozen emails suggesting revisions in format as well as content. Then, in this age of email and online you will often hear from someone who disagrees with your ideas. In the scholarly conversation, the strongest ideas survive, some weaker ideas are made stronger, some weak ideas die, and some of the best are piggybacked upon to become dominant concepts in the field. Isn't it interesting how some professorial martinets terrorize students dependent upon the instructor for a grade, but never submit their wonderful ideas into the marketplace for evaluation?

Six, in an era when Kern, Mettetal, Dixson, and Morgan (2015) claim, "Both accreditation and state funding formulas are increasingly linked to evidence of student learning" (p. 10), **SoTL provides a methodology for your work helping your institution with funding and accreditation**. Moreover, when your institution works on such things as strategic plans, you have offered them proof of what works, and you may help your own department set up an evidence-based rubric for promotion and tenure.

Possible SoTL Article Types

Nelson (2016) lists thirteen types of SoTL articles:

1. It Worked

2. Before & After: Qualitative Assessments of Changes in Practice

3. Before & After: Quantitative Assessments of Changes

4. Developing Good Ideas

5. Summaries of Expert Knowledge Gained by Self-Reflection and Experimentation in Ones [sic] Own Teaching

6. Integration of Larger Frameworks with Classroom Practice

7. Qualitative Studies Designed to Explore a Key Issue

8. Quantitative Comparisons of Different Courses or Sections

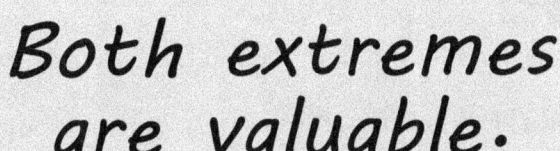

9. Comparisons of a Wide Array of Different Courses Using a Common Assessment Instrument

10. Experimental Analyses

11. Annotated Bibliographies

12. Brief, Annotated Summaries of Key Research Findings

13. Formal (Quantitative) Meta-Analyses.

Eight-Step Approach to SoTL

On their website, Indiana University offers an eight-step approach to creating a SoTL article that parallels our model in a previous chapter:

1. Read the literature.

2. Write the literature review.

3. Create a research question or hypothesis.

4. Choose a research method.

5. Analyze your data.

6. Draw conclusions.

7. Write the paper.

8. Submit the paper to a conference/publication.

On the other hand, Savory, Burnett, and Goodburn (2007) posit a simpler approach: "In general, there are four major steps to carrying out an effective classroom inquiry: formulating an inquiry question, developing an assessment strategy, evaluating the results of your study, and drawing conclusions and recommendations from these results" (p. 7).

Problems with SoTl

While we advocate very strongly for SoTL, we recognize it perils.

One, **SoTL is still an infant field** not fully grown enough for some disciplines and departments. As a result, tenure and promotion committees may not recognize what you have wrought. According to Beach, Sorcinelli, Austin, and Rivard (2016), SoTL ranks a distant 13th on a list of Top Issues Faculty Development Should Address in the Next Five Years (p. 173).

Two, **some disciplines will recognize only research in that field**, and not all SoTL research is discipline specific, thankfully.

Three, **SoTL alone does not guarantee superior teaching**. As Kern, Mettetal, Dixson, and Morgan (2015) state, "Although SoTL might be included in the teaching portfolio, it should not be necessary or considered sufficient to demonstrate excellence in teaching" (p. 9).

Four, **sometimes the SoTL central idea in your article is better than your evidence**. What this means is you need help from experts in the field to suggest ways in which you can go. We admit to once having a great idea about teaching new faculty without knowing how to assess it. As a result, we turned to assessment guru Peggy Maki and asked her advice when she came to our college to conduct a workshop. Not only did she offer some effective strategies, but our discussion led to a major collaborative article.

Five, **some scholars doubt the SoTL methodology.** As Hutchings and Shulman (1999) state, "Many believe that it [SoTL] will not be well received by those in my discipline because it does not use 'credible' methods of inquiry" (p. 14).

As a result, before practicing SoTL with an eye toward promotion/tenure, check to see what your home department values. And don't think you will become a SoTL expert overnight. We did not start to publish in faculty development extensively until we had spent almost 10 years in the field, thus verifying Ericsson, Krampe, and Tesch-Romer's (1993) theory of **deliberate practice**.

Conclusion

Indeed, the scholarship of teaching and learning provides you with some unique opportunities and challenges when compared with Boyer's other categories. Perhaps its greatest advantage for you, however, is the ability to meld two of the three areas vital to your academic success, teaching and scholarly productivity. Further, because the field is so new with so many journals, it affords you a chance to position yourself as an expert and rise as the field takes on increasing significance.

References

Beach, A., Sorcinelli, M., Austin, A., & Rivard, J. (2016). *Faculty development in the age of evidence: Current practices, future imperatives.* Sterling, VA: Stylus.

Blythe, H. & Sweet, C. (2004). Total team teaching. *The Teaching Professor*, 18(3), 1-3.

Blythe, H. & Sweet, C. (2008). Keeping your class C.R.I.S.P. *NEA Higher Education Advocate*, 26(2), 5-8.

Boyer, E. (1990). *Scholarship reconsidered: Priorities of the professoriate.* San Francisco: Jossey-Bass.

Carnegie Foundation. (2001). Retrieved from the Carnegie Foundation website: https://www.carnegiefoundation.org

Ericsson, K., Ktampe, R., & Tesch-Romer, C. (1993). The role of deliberate practice in the acquisition of expert performance. *Psychological Review*, 100(3), 363-406.

Friberg, J. (2016). Framing SoTL: Understanding the scholarship of teaching and learning and its role in CSD: Part 1. Retrieved from American Speech-Language-Hearing Association website: http://www.asha.org/Academic/questions/Framing-SoTL-Part 1/

Hutchings, P. & Shulman, L. (1999). The scholarship of teaching: New elaborations, new developments. *Change*, 31(5), 11-15.

Indiana University. (2016). SoTL 101. Retrieved from the Faculty Academy on Excellence in Teaching website: https://facet.iu.edu/sotl/sotl-101/

Kern, B., Mettetal, G., Dixson, M. & Morgan, R. (2015, June). The role of SoTL in the academy: Upon the 25th anniversary of Boyer's *scholarship reconsidered*. *Journal of the Scholarship for Teaching and Learning,* 15(3), 1-14. doi: 10.14434/josotl.v15i3.13623

McKinney, K. (2004). The scholarship of teaching and learning: Past lessons, current challenges and future visions. In C M. Wehlburg & S. Chadwick-Blossey (Eds.), *To Improve the Academy* (Vol. 22, pp. 3-19). Boston, MA: Anker.

Miller-Young, J. (2015, February 11). How to tell the story of SoTL. Retrieved from http://blogs.mtroyal.ca/isptl/2015/02/11/how-to-tell-the-story-of-sotl/

Nelson, C. (2016). How could I do scholarship of teaching & learning? Retrieved from http://php.indiana.edu/~nelson1/TCHNGBKS.html/

Savory, P., Burnett, A., & Goodburn, A. (2007). *Inquiry into the college classroom: A journey toward scholarly teaching.* Bolton, MA: Anker.

Sweet, C., Blythe, H., Phillips, B., & Daniel, C. (2014). *Achieving excellence in teaching: A self-help guide.* Stillwater: New Forums.

Weimer, M. (2006). *Enhancing scholarly work on teaching & learning.* San Francisco: Jossey-Bass.

Weimer, M. (2015). A `best of' list that celebrates the scholarship of teaching & learning. Retrieved from *The Teaching Professor* Blog website: http://www.facultyfocus.com/articles/teaching-professor-blog/best-list-celebrates-scholar/

2
Beginning the Ascent

IX. GENERATING IDEAS

As long-time conference presenters in fiction and nonfiction, the four of us have discovered that conferees pepper us with two main questions: how do you guys write together, and where do you get so many ideas? While the collaboration issue will be treated in a later chapter, the question of idea generation seems pertinent at this juncture. While questioners seem to be asking us the question, what they're really seeking is successful strategies for generating their own works. The importance of idea generation is underscored by the fact that invention (*inventio*) is one of the five canons (categories) of classical rhetoric.

All the best-laid plans we've discussed so far—developing a scholarly frame of mind, engaging in market analysis, and becoming disciplined in your approach to writing production—matter little if you are unable to generate ideas with scholarly value. Like a climber with an adventurous mindset who has studied the mountain ahead and prepared for the climb, you are destined to remain at the bottom of the slopes without an assault plan you can successfully carry out. In short, you not only have to learn how to write, but how to find ideas to write about.

In *Options* (2013) Hal and Charlie provide one of their favorite maxims to stress the importance of form in fiction—"You can't make Jell-O without a mold." The converse is equally true. The best mold in the world remains useless without Jell-O or a good idea to fill it. In fact, the failure to generate ideas is one of the chief causes of writer's block and hence the lack of scholarly production. Fortunately, not one of us has ever suffered from the inability to begin, so we're ready to share our strategies. Ideas for scholarly production come from a number of sources.

Invention Strategies

Read. As we suggested in an earlier chapter, **the number one source for ideas is reading.** In fact, we heartily agree with the statement that a good writer must first be a good reader. How many newspapers do you read daily either in paper or online format? Rusty starts every day at 6:00 a.m. with a menu of Fruit Loops and three-four blogs. Charlie always has a novel going that he sometimes reads even during TV commercials and certainly while watching baseball, looking at the tube only when the crowd roars. Bill reads multiple books at a time and keeps them on a table next to his favorite chair, and Hal often spends his afternoons delving into books on mythology. Despite having an office next to the campus library, Hal and Charlie each subscribe

Dickinson's Law—There is no frigate like a book.

to three journals. One of Hal and Charlie's favorite pieces of literary criticism came about because they were reading a book by Charlie's grandmother wherein she told a story of hunting with Phil Percival, Ernest Hemingway's favorite guide (Phil told both Papa and Granny the same hunting tale, and Hemingway turned it into a classic short story).

Mark what you read. Every book Charlie owns, including fiction, has been marked up with underlines, marginal notations, and question marks. Every book in Hal and Charlie's office has yellow plumes of paper rising from its top like chimney smoke. On the yellow markers are written various comments. Bill tends to write key words in the margins and summarize ideas at the end of each chapter, and Rusty keeps a sort of reading diary that only he understands. To simply read is passive; to mark is active. Every single mark is a potential seed for an article, book, or story.

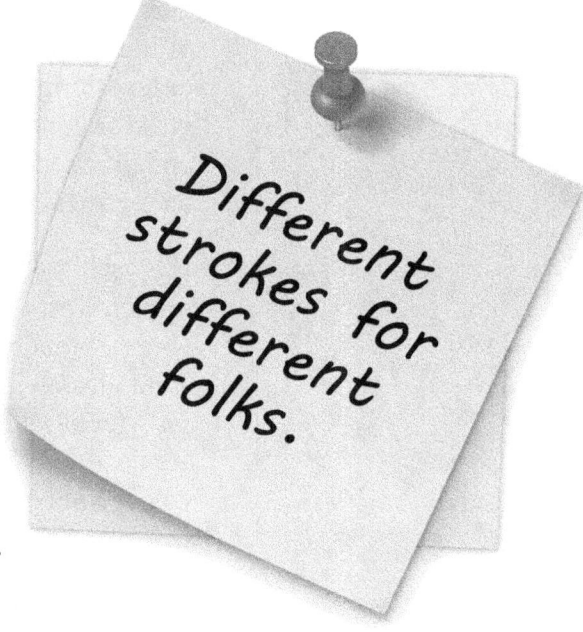

Stephen King believes that all writers have filters that help them sift out the wheat from the chaff in daily experience. We believe that **over time your developing scholarly frame of mind becomes a filter.** And this filter isn't limited to academic publications; even when you're reading an issue of *Southern Living* or *Fine Homebuilding*, your mind is hepa-filtering out particles that have future use. For instance, one article Hal and Charlie published in a book came about as a reaction to a *New York Times* piece by William Safire.

Make notes on movies and TV programs. A few years back Hal was watching his favorite, The History Channel, when he saw a fascinating show on the Nazi *wunderwaffen*. When our creative community sat down to plot a novel, he found his notes on a super weapon from World War II around which a contemporary novel could be based.

Think of the **classes** you teach as idea incubators. In rereading John Cheever's "The Swimmer" before class one day, Charlie continued to write in his textbook and gradually noticed a pattern emerging in his comments. For his dissertation Charlie had written about Bernard Malamud's use of the imagery of the grail quest, so while he didn't exactly milk his dissertation, he did see an emerging grail pattern in Cheever's story. In another class a student asked Hal about the use of a specific word, "agape," in Coleridge's "The Rime of the Ancient Mariner." Not knowing the answer, Hal promised to get back to the student. Later in a discussion when Charlie said the word out loud Hal heard it not as a facial description but as a Christian celebration (the love feast). A little investigation produced an answer for the student and a publication for Hal and Charlie.

Apply research in one field to another. On a nine-month contract, Charlie used to support his family during the summers by doing carpentry work. After reading books and magazines on how to accomplish such things as building a deck, Charlie applied his avocational interest of carpentry to his vocation of teaching literature. As a result, he began to examine structures such as Hawthorne's house of Seven Gables and Poe's house of Usher, which resulted in many publications. As an undergraduate, Charlie became enamored with the philosophy of existentialism. Whenever he needed a paper in graduate school, his fallback position was "An Existential Interpretation of [insert any literary work]." Later, this love for the 60s'-popular philosophy melded with Hal's undergraduate work with John Killinger, the noted expert in the field, to produce an article on door imagery, "Existentialism in Hemingway's 'The Killers.'"

Pay attention to what colleagues say. Obviously, when one is part of a writing tetrad, three other people are available to bounce ideas off. Charlie and Hal once heard the professor in the office next to them talking about how the openings of Browning's poems are reflected in the closings. As they were teaching Browning in their World Lit class, they immediately brought up the idea to the class and asked for their help in analyzing three Browning poems for the colleague's pattern. One time Hal made a comment about one of Poe's narrator's strange habit of pulling the teeth out of dead women. "Must be afraid she's a vampire who's going to come back from the grave and bite him" or something to the effect. They both laughed at the pop culture interpretation, but both remembered the comment well enough to build a logical argument around Hal's thesis that came to fruition in an article for *Poe Studies*.

Be a fly on the wall. Everyone likes to eavesdrop, especially in public places like airports and restaurants. Admittedly, this source offers more uses for creative writers who can glom on words and phrases. Charlie and Hal once built an entire short story around an overheard dialectical pronunciation of service (tree) as "sarfas." Uncle Bob's anecdote about opening a place called A Bar with No Name also provides fodder for fiction. On the other hand, have you ever been sitting at a conference bar (coffee or adult beverage) and heard somebody say something? As noted earlier, the best advice Charlie ever got on writing came in just such a place when his chair looked up from a drink he was nursing and said, "There isn't a school in America you can't write your way into—or out of." At the famed Lilly Conference during a session break Hal and Charlie heard the person at the next table mentioning "instructional alignment." They introduced themselves to L. Dee Fink a/k/a Fink and the conference co-director, they began talking, brought an idea back to Rusty, and a published article on the four Rs of deep learning resulted.

Adapt what you are given. Hal and Charlie published several articles in *The Writer* and *Writer's Digest* on subjects they initially knew little about. Editors kept pitching ideas at them with the tag question, "Can you give me 1500-words on Subject X?" One editor at a mystery magazine had a collection of potential pictures for the cover, and it was cheaper for him to use these pictures for covers than to commission new covers, so he sent them to Hal and Charlie, saying he would print any story they would write that reflected the pictures. The first, a painting of a gorilla in the treetops, became "Terror Island." Another time they received a panicked call from a friend who edited a journal of notes on contemporary literature, a periodical to which they often contributed. He had promised a special issue devoted to Salinger's *The Catcher in the Rye*, but had received only five acceptable pieces and needed five more. Hal and Charlie wrote him six pieces of scholarly gold in the space of a week.

Write about what you know ... differently. As you might suspect from our examples of Charlie writing for *TV Guide* and Hal watching The History Channel, we like television. Our wasted time in front of the boob tube has led us to research on educational television and several publications in journals such as *College English*. Charlie even published an article in the 80s on satellite television and his beloved New York Giants. Charlie, a child in the birth of rock and roll, believes the greatest rock song ever written is Don McLean's "American Pie." Instead of just singing bye, bye to a lost era of music, he researched the song, created his own mini-casebook of it, and used the casebook in his first-year English classes for years as a way of introducing research. Hal, who has reared on the Rolling Stones, never agreed with him, but liked the methodology. Together they published an article on the mini-casebook approach to teaching research.

Keep a file of things that interest you even if you don't know why they do so. Rusty's trusty Apple laptop has hundreds of articles, pictures, and news items that he might want to use someday. Hal and Charlie are more old-fashioned and keep a clip file. They tear items out of newspapers (before their wives have read them) and rip items from magazines. One such tear-out on dangerous plants was applied to those the Reverend Dimmesdale is exposed to in *The Scarlet Letter*, thereby explaining some of his weird behavior. When they were getting paid to ghostwrite the Mike Shayne series, they became bored after a year. One day early in his career while teaching *The Scarlet Letter*, Charlie noticed a time discrepancy in the novel's chronology, jotted down a short note about it, and threw it in the file. Twenty years later he mentioned it to Hal, and they found the note, examined the mistake in chronology in detail, and published a scholarly note on the flaw in Hawthorne's masterpiece.

Generate one idea per day, which is our previous guideline on steroids. **Don't wait for ideas to come to you—instead, seek them out.** Meetings and classes should suggest new ideas. And don't forget about reading, whether it's something you spot on your daily viewing of the Internet (including social media) or that material on the table beside your favorite chair. We answer over 80 emails/day, and we tell ourselves that if we can find one good idea in them, then the whole email process is worth it. We read at least one article/day and always have a book beside us. Right now, for instance, we're perusing *Faculty Development in the Age of Evidence*, *Coming in from the Margins*, and John Sandford's latest Lucas Dav-

> *The best defense is a good offense.*

enport thriller. We write a blog post for New Forums every Monday morning, and those topics emerge from a list of ideas that sits on Charlie's desk. Not only is nothing wasted on us, but we actively use those ideas that register on our minds.

Yesterday, for example, Hal and Charlie were watching football, and ads kept appearing for Amazon's Echo and Google Home, virtual assistants. Yes, we became annoyed with their repetition, but it also struck us that the new device might make an excellent focal point for a mystery story. Stephen King says that all stories come from the convergence of two ideas, and we happened to recall Henry II's query about Thomas More, "Will no one rid me of this meddlesome priest?" that led to the priest's death. Suppose someone were to say to Alexa, "Would someone rid me of this tiresome wife?" Would the blue ring atop the cylinder light up as Alexa sprang into action? By coincidence or synchronicity, the next day we picked up the new issue of *Kiplinger's Personal Finance* (January 2017), and there on page 37 was an article called "Alexa, at Your Command." Fate, we think not.

Another Approach to Creativity

Rather than following our guidelines, you might want to approach the germination phase of writing from the angle of creativity. In our *Introduction to Applied Creative Thinking* (2012), Rusty, Charlie, and Hal surveyed the field of creative thinking and reduced the various strategies uncovered to what they called the "nifty nine." While these strategies do not exhaust the field, they do represent its most fundamental and powerful concepts. In fact, if you analyze the nine just-presented guidelines, you'll see how some of them overlap the "nifty nine" (the two nonets are purely coincidental . . . or are they?):

1. **Shifting Perception** "involves looking at a person, idea, or situation from a new perspective" (p. 28). Did you notice in the first paragraph how we shifted from our perception of a phenomenon to that of people asking us for the source of our ideas? When we discussed being a fly on the wall, we explained how we looked at things from other's perspectives. The article on "The Rime of the Ancient Mariner" Hal and Charlie published in *The Wordsworth Circle* came directly from a shift in perspective on a familiar word.

2. **Piggybacking** is "borrowing old ideas from others in order to form new ideas" (p. 33). In essence, all literary criticism demands one piggyback on what previous critics have said. Sometimes we even piggyback off ourselves as when Hal and Charlie published a dozen articles on John Cheever's "The Swimmer." Each separate piece built on the one before it.

3. **Brainstorming** is a process that allows you to "generate lots of ideas; quantity is initially more important than quality" (p. 36). Hal and Charlie used to call their office "The Green Room," a reference to the room in which guests wait before their appearances on talk shows. Many of the articles originated as they brainstormed in the office before and after classes.

4. **Glimmer-catching**: "a glimmer is that out-of-focus object in the corner of your eye, barely perceptible sound, or fuzz idea that is the start of a larger idea" (p. 44). Remember the narrator of Poe's "Berenice" pulling teeth or the overheard comment on Browning?

5. **Collaborating**: "Twenty-five years ago initial studies found that collaboration increased ideation by 60-70%. Then a few years ago we read a business article that suggested that three or more collaborators could raise that rate to 400-700% (p. 46). There are four of us in this configuration, but we've published pieces with seven co-authors on assessment. We saw a statistic that the number of authors on a publication in scientific journals has doubled over the last 25 years.

6. **Going with the Flow** is the total involvement in the act of creativity that displaces self-consciousness, distractions, and time (pp. 52-53). Oftentimes, Charlie will get an idea and start tapping away on his desktop computer. Hal has learned to keep quiet until the muse releases his officemate. One advantage to the computer is that it allows the writer [suppose at the end of Mason's "Shiloh" that Norma's flapping of her arms is an image of a bird taking off from its nest] to immediate capture a glimmer and freeze it forever in print.

7. **Playing** "is a state of mind that kindles our openness to the world around us" (p. 59). All four of us play the game of "What If" quite frequently. The rules of the game are simple. Participants throw out the wildest ideas they come up with, and like an improv troupe, the others in the room say "Yes . . . and"—i.e., they keep it alive by building on it. Eventually the idea grows strong enough to live, or it dies from its own lack of weight or absurdity.

8. **Recognizing Pattern** "is the ability to discern the figure in the carpet by weaving together separate strands into a coherent whole." (p. 64). When we wrote earlier in the chapter to "Write about what you know" and connected it to our *TV Guide* example before that, we were recognizing a pattern. Hal and Charlie wrote a seminal note on the narrator of Faulkner's "A Rose for Emily" by first noting the narrator's use of chivalric imagery in the story's opening. Spotting that image helped them spot the next, and, voila, an article.

9. **Using Metaphor** "is an effective creative strategy for learning about the unknown and gaining a perspective on it" (p. 67). Go back to our Introduction chapter, and at its beginning find the poem on "The Assistant

Professor." When it was being written, that poem grew from a simple comparison between the assistant professor and an octopus and then expanded those similarities. The result is an extended metaphor that helps illuminate the struggle toward tenure. And what about the major extended metaphor that blends this book into a coherent whole? At the book's inception we began with the staircase metaphor we had used in a previous book, but found the staircase did not sufficiently express the rigor necessary to achieve scholarly productivity.

Conclusion

You've doubtless noticed that both of our nonet schemes for generating ideas have some overlap. If we were to synthesize them both, we would simply quote again Henry James' advice to a would-be writer: **"Try to be one of those people on whom nothing is lost."**

X. FOLLOWING THE TRAIL OF THE TYPICAL RESEARCH ARTICLE

Recently, Bill hiked a mountain trail that had a wooden sign engraved with a map at the beginning, was marked with white blazes on trees along the way, and was well worn. Thus easy to follow, the trail led to a spectacular view of a double arch in Kentucky's Red River Gorge. Likewise, the ascent to the top of the mountain of publication of the typical research article is much easier when a trail is followed. **Even small steps in the right direction make progress over time if the trail is visible.** Depending on the specific discipline, research articles vary in style, but the following is an example of one major format that can be tweaked for most disciplines. The trail begins with 1) an **abstract**, which leads the reader to 2) an **introduction**, through 3) a **literature review**, 4) a **methodology**, 5) **findings**, 6) a **discussion**, and ends with 7) a **conclusion**.

1. Abstract. As discussed in an earlier chapter, the abstract is a succinct paragraph about the purpose and implications of the study. Because the abstract provides the reasons the article should be read, it may be the only thing that is read. Often when researchers are perusing articles, only the abstracts are read to determine the relevant work that needs to be examined closer. Also, the submission guidelines for a presentation usually ask only for an abstract and a title to be submitted. Therefore, a well-written abstract is essential. According to Calabrese (2009), the abstract should include a brief overview of the following five key components of the study:

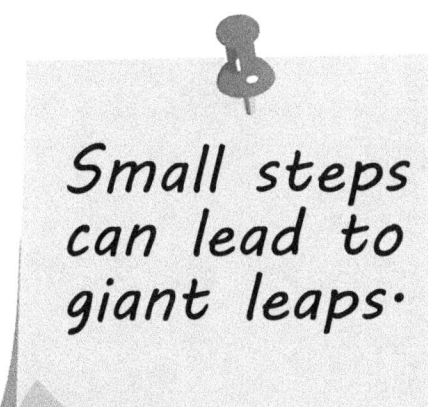

Small steps can lead to giant leaps.

- **Problem statement**. The problem statement describes an issue and tells why it is important. The problem statement is often a condition that is perplexing or a conflict that offers choices for a resolution. A solution cannot be identified until a problem is well defined. A problem statement might ask, "As Eastern Kentucky University is improving the retention of first-year students, what are the variables that are effecting this change?"

- **Research questions**. Research questions or hypotheses specifically address the problem statement. Writers should choose one or the other, not both. Research questions will ask who, what, when, or why? Hypotheses make a calculated guess at the findings. Research questions are used more with qualitative studies, while hypotheses are employed mostly with quantitative studies.

- **Methodology.** A brief paragraph on methodology describes the big picture of the procedures used to collect data to answer the statement of the problem and research questions or hypotheses.

- **Findings.** Findings or results are logical conclusions flowing from the data analysis free from interpretation. The results must relate directly to the problem statement and the research questions or hypothesis. For example, "The results of this study revealed that financial support was the key predictor of student retention. An examination of the descriptive data offered the following major conclusions: the ACT was a significant predictor of student retention, the association with athletics was a significant predictor of student retention, and high school grade point average was not a significant predictor of student retention."

- **Implications.** A statement about future research, policy, and practical application should be included in the abstract and expanded on in the conclusions. For example, "Now that predictors of retention have been identified in this study, future research needs to be conducted to determine programs and policies that have an effect on retention."

The method undergirds the message.

2. Introduction. The introduction ensures alignment with all components of the article. It serves the purpose of telling the reader what can be expected to come forth from the article. For example, Bill often will read the introduction and the conclusion of an article to determine if the research is relevant. Does the research support the line of thinking pursued in a new study? It is a fast way for the reader to peruse a whole stack of research studies when conducting a review of literature. The introduction needs to include the following components."

- **Objectives and aims.** The objectives and aims answer the question of why the research is important. Objectives and aims of the study flow from a metacognitive reflection on the problem statement and the research questions. According to Calabrese (2009), the two following questions may help with the reflection: What needs to be accomplished to further this scholarly discussion, and what are the desired outcomes?

- **Assumptions.** Assumptions are stated to give perspective and knowledge about speculations that may have influenced the scholarly conversation. Underlying assumptions adopted from previous research and theories often determine the direction of the study (Myers 1997).

- **Limitations.** Any perceived limitations that might occur before the study begins should be stated. By examining the study for flaws before the study begins, the author becomes more respectful of results, and the scholarly conversation becomes more valid. With limitations addressed, findings become indications, not final proof of a causal relationship.

- **Significance**. In the introduction the significance of a study speculates on importance. It answers one of the following questions. Why is this study significant? How does it contribute to the scholarly conversation? Does it support a theoretical construct? Might it be used to implement new policies?

- **Key terms**. The definition of key terms should be included to avoid multiple interpretations of words. Clarity is important so that key words are not misconstrued. When appropriate, citations should be included to justify the definition used.

3. Literature Review. A review of the relevant literature establishes a conceptual theoretical framework for the study. Relevant literature is any knowledge that is important to the new study. It identifies for the reader the historical links to new ideas (Burke 2001). All truth stands on the shoulders of scholars who came before; therefore, no article should be written in a vacuum. A review of literature attempts to link old knowledge to new thoughts by citing previously published authors. The following are components of a review of literature to consider:

- **Conceptual framework**. The conceptual framework is a map detailing the approach to be used to summit the mountain. All mountains have different paths to the top, and so it is with research studies; one can approach them from different angles. The conceptual framework outlines the approach step by step of how the author conceptualizes the study and gives theoretical perspective through a review of literature (Krumme 2000).

- **Theoretical considerations**. The review of literature takes into consideration the works of theorists who have blazed the trail the researcher chooses to follow. The rationale for the research design is supported with a review of literature that includes a synopsis of the writings of these theorists. It includes explicit theoretical constructs that focus all good research (Yin 2003).

- **Criteria**. What are the criteria used to review relevant literature? How were articles selected or rejected? What are the limitations to existing studies? What gaps become apparent? These are the questions researchers need to ask and report on when conducting a thorough review of literature.

- **Synthesis**. Once the review of appropriate literature has been completed then relevant findings and conclusions should be drawn. These conclusions should include anything learned about the conceptual framework, the theoretical considerations, the limitations, and the gaps.

4. Methodology. The methodology section describes in detail the research processes and procedures used by the author in such a way that the study could be replicated (Calabrese 2009). Replication is key to the scientific method because multiple studies using the same processes and procedures help to establish a pattern of variables that create significance. **Stating the precise methods used to conduct the research establishes the validity and reliability of the conclusions drawn.** The methodology should include the following five components: the purpose of the study, research questions, data collection, analysis, and any inherent biases.

- **Purpose**. The purpose of the study provides the reader with a concise summation of argument. According to Calabrese (2009), the following questions are important to answer when describing the purpose: What is the problem to be investigated? What is the population studied? By gaining an understanding of this problem, what might be gained?

- **Questions**. State three or four research questions or hypotheses that will add to the scholarly conversation concerning the problem identified. Research questions are questions and hypotheses are statements. For example, a research question might be, "What financial issues influence the retention of first year students at Eastern Kentucky University?" A hypothesis might be phrased, "Financial issues are the most important variable for retaining first year students at Eastern Kentucky University." Research questions or hypotheses help determine the methods needed to conduct a study.

- **Data collection**. "The data collection section describes the methods, procedures, and characteristics of the sample" (Calabrese, 2009, p.38). It begins with the purpose of the study, identifies the population, variables, and data collection techniques. For example, "The purpose of this study is to determine the variables effecting student retention at Eastern Kentucky University. A focus group of students was randomly selected from orientation courses offered by EKU. The focus group identified a list of predictors that they thought influenced their retention. A review of literature confirmed the validity of the list of predictors and a questionnaire was created. An IRB proposal was written, submitted, and approved to survey all first year students at EKU."

- **Analysis**. A statement about analysis of the data is then given. For example, "The multiple linear regression technique, utilizing multiple correlation and analysis of covariance was used to test the hypotheses. Descriptive data including means, number, and percentages were calculated for all predictor variables."

- **Biases**. According to Patton (2002), identifying conditions that may lead to bias in the research is important. A statement should be included describing how the scholar insured neutrality while directing the study.

5. Findings. After the purpose of the study has been postulated, research questions have been identified, data have been collected and analyzed, findings can be stated. Begin by restating each research question or hypothesis and then write about what the analyzed data indicate without interpretation. At this point the scholar should not speculate on what the data mean. As the TV detective said, **"Just state the facts, only the facts."** Accurate publication of the findings in a straightforward manner provides integrity for the study.

A technical point to remember is that research questions have findings while hypotheses have results. Regardless of what they are called, they are treated the same. Both can use charts if they help present the results in more detail. Both results and findings just state the facts.

6. Discussion. Now that the results have been stated in a straightforward manner without interpretation, opinions and speculations can be stated openly and honestly. When Charles Darwin collected data on the Galapagos Islands, he wrote about the results of the data in several books before he had an open discussion about his opinions in *The Origin of the Species* (1859). It took Darwin twenty-five years of cogitation to interpret and speculate on the data before he wrote a theory about how and why species evolve. This section should include an open discussion about the findings and scholarly discussion of what might be made of the results. Future research and new theories can be postulated in this section as well. The author should conclude with any shortcomings of the study and why the findings are significant (Skelton and Edwards 2000). The following should be included:

- **Scholarly discussion.** The whole purpose for conducting research is to have a scholarly discussion in writing that can be shared broadly. Why did the study produce the results? How does this study relate to the body of knowledge on the topic? What are the strengths and weaknesses of the results of the study?

- **Implications.** Implications should address the following three questions: Who cares about the results and why? What are future research questions that might be considered? Might there be new theoretical perspectives or policy?

- **Shortcomings.** After the research has been conducted, write a sentence on shortcomings. This review of the study opens the door to possible shortcomings of methodologies used and provides proof that any research design may be flawed. For example, "This study began with a small focus group to identify possible variables pertaining to retention of first year students. This might be a shortcoming of the study and could be improved by including a larger sample size."

- **Significance.** In the conclusion the paragraph on significance states why the study was meaningful to this line of inquiry. How did it add to the knowledge base and how does it relate to the conceptual framework?

7. Conclusion. The conclusion summarizes the key points, the salient issues, and the significance of the key findings. It states the outcomes and their impact on the ongoing scholarly discussion on the topic and speculates on future research questions. Provide the reader with a succinct paragraph summarizing the article without reference to any new or extraneous material.

References

Burke, C. (2001). The doctoral dissertation proposal. Retrieved November 8, 2016, from http://www.usc.edu/schoools/sppd/private/document/doctoral/resources.pdf/

Calabrese, R. (2009). *The dissertation desk reference.* Plymouth, UK: Rowan & Littlefield Education.

Krumme, G. (2000). Phases, stages, and steps in geographic investigation & research. Retrieved November 7, 2016, from http://faculty.washignton.edu/krumme/guides/researchguide.html

Myers, M. (1997). Qualitative research in information systems. *MIS Quarterly*, 21(2), 241-242.

Patton, M.Q. (2002). *Qualitative research & evaluation methods* (3rd ed.). Thousand Oaks: Sage.

Skelton, J. & and Edwards, S. (2000). The function of the discussion section in academic medical writing. *British Medical Journal,* 320(7244), 1269-1270.

Yin, R. (2003). *Case study research: Design and methods* (3rd ed.). Thousand Oaks, CA: Sage.

3

Into Thin Air

XI. COLLABORATION WITH COLLEAGUES AND STUDENTS

Pierre & Marie Curie, Rodgers & Hart, Currier & Ives, you and ? The potential for collaboration is an important consideration for any writing project. Collaboration is a strategy that can involve faculty colleagues and students. This chapter offers a rationale for why collaboration is important, an overview of successful faculty collaborations, and perspectives on successful faculty-student collaborations. For a view of collaboration—and proof that collaboration works—from a creative perspective, check out Chapter 10 of our *Introduction to Applied Creative Thinking* (Stillwater: New Forums, 2012).

Rationale

Collaboration can enhance the quantity and quality of writing, allow for new research perspectives, and serve as learning and growth opportunities. Many of the most successful research projects were developed through collaboration. While researchers and writers in the sciences have long engaged in collaborations (sometimes with over a dozen authors), humanities researchers are learning to design collaborative partnerships that enhance their work as well.

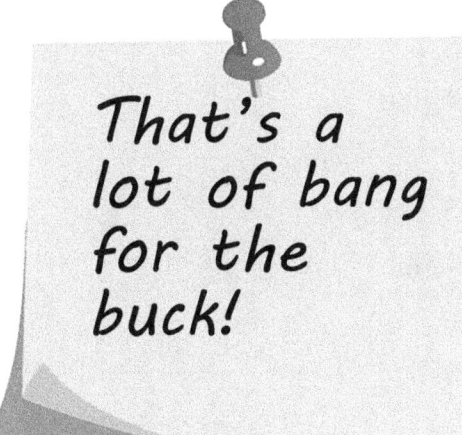

Collaboration is an important strategy for maximizing your scholarly productivity because it:

- Can decrease the amount of time to produce writing;

- Can increase ideational levels over 700%;

- Can offer opportunities for piggybacking;

- Can use others' strengths to compensate for writers' weaknesses;

- Can expand perspectives for generating content, revising, and editing;

- Can defeat the essential loneliness of research by providing a socializing opportunity;
- Can build ongoing research teams;
- Can provide additional perspectives; and
- Can add research dimensions.

We'll examine three perspectives on collaborative relationships:

- Faculty-Faculty Collaborations,
- Faculty-Student Collaborations,
- Collaborative Technologies.

Faculty-Faculty Collaborations

Why does collaboration matter? In our experience, both the research and teaching processes can be enhanced. Students benefit from authentic, research-based learning experiences with focused, experienced faculty, while faculty learn from the perspectives, questions, and concepts offered by their peers. Faculty collaborating with faculty colleagues can find it advantageous to share their research, data, and approaches across departments or academic institutions. Rusty, for instance, collaborates with faculty members from the west coast and around the country. Hal and Charlie have co-written and team taught for over forty years. Just counting configurations for New Forums' books, Hal and Charlie have collaborated with Rusty, Bill, Shawn Apostel, and Chris Daniel.

Highly effective faculty collaborations are built on mutual respect, assigned duties, and agreed-upon timelines. Let's begin with a few questions to consider before entering into a collaborative writing experience.

- Does the research-focus of the project require additional expertise?
- Would the style of the manuscript benefit from an additional writer or team of writers?
- Is the project substantial enough to involve more faculty coauthors?
- Do you have access to willing and capable coauthors with the background, ability, and expertise you need?
- Do you have colleagues with whom you already engage in successful collaborations?
- How would you define successful collaboration for this scholarly project?

Consider Table 1 as you decide the best option for collaboration in this project.

Table 1. Collaboration Options

Project	*Status*	*Expertise Needed*	*Potential Co-authors*

Not all projects are ideal for collaboration, and it's critical that you make this decision early in the process. In addition, your institute, even a specific journal, might preference single-author publications over collaborative-authored work.

Consider options and priorities when making authorship decisions. Ordering of authors says something about the manuscript and your contributions. For example, first author (commonly referred to as the lead author) suggests that this author has taken the lead on the manuscript and has given the most effort or was the originator of the manuscript or research. Second author does not automatically suggest less effort. It can indicate equal authorship or a support role. The same is true for third, fourth, and other authorship ordering. Depending on institutional expectations, authorship can be more (or less) important. Many research-based and teaching institutions value productive scholarly co-author teams, while others might recommend that faculty have at least one major, single-authored publication. In some cases, single-author, major, peer-reviewed publications might be the priority. See Table 2.

As we pointed out earlier, then, successful collaborations require several elements:

- Mutual respect;

- Assigned duties;

- Clear expectations; and

- Agreed-upon timelines.

While many collaborations work out as planned and are considered productive, we must also consider the pitfalls of collaboration. These issues commonly prevent successful writing efforts, result in delays, and detract from productivity. Common pitfalls include:

- Lack of clearly stated short-term, intermediate, and long-term writing goals;

- Personality conflicts;

- Co-authors or researchers who are not committed to the writing process or project;

- Writers with less expertise than first thought;

- Nonresponsive co-authors; and

- Technology and tools-related issues that complicate collaboration.

Regardless of your institution's authorship recommendations and expectations for publication, be able to explain and justify author ordering in collaborative authorship teams. In some cases, the second author might have given most effort in the publication, but the lead author originated the idea or took the lead in securing the book contract, for example. We suggest being able to explain your authorship role, regardless of where you fall in line. In addition, we encourage you to work out those agreements and details in advance. When Rusty was going up for tenure, we encouraged him to take the lead on books and articles so that his name would appear first in the credit line. After seven books and over twenty-five articles, we have never found order of authorship to be an issue. In fact, the lead author is most often determined by who has the most time at the moment and who has the greatest expertise.

Faculty-Student Collaborations

We often see students as students in the classroom with lives outside of the academy once they leave our doors. While successful teaching in the classroom is critical to any major academic institution, faculty-student collaboration and co-authorship often go unnoticed and, even when acknowledged, underappreciated.

Undergraduate research programs and scholarly celebrations of student work, like research poster showcases, offer a productive model for highly collaborative faculty-student co-authorship. At our own institution, we collaborate regularly with our office, Undergraduate Research and Creative Endeavors. This program has grown from around 75 research poster submissions to well over 100 in a short time. In addition, this office launched the *Kentucky Journal of Undergraduate Scholarship*. Both venues—one focused on presentation and the other publication—provide opportunities for students and faculty to collaborate on major scholarly work important to the academic institution and to the process of learning.

Higher education is undergoing major shifts. In the process, we're constantly updating and rethinking approaches to teaching and learning. Meanwhile, faculty development has taken center stage at many higher education institutions across the country and internationally. The convergence of both areas suggests a shift in the landscape of faculty production, blurring lines previously delineating classroom teaching and lab-based research. With the proliferation of the Association of American Colleges and Universities' High-Impact Practices (see www.aacu.org/leap/hips) as priorities at major institutions and an emphasis on innovation (see University Innovation Alliance at www/theuia.org), some of the most important discoveries—those that are publication and presentation worthy—are happening among highly engaged and supremely committed and talented students. **When paired with savvy and successful faculty, students can produce some of the most innovative scholarship available.** Team-based authorship and research can make for powerful production models that also exploit High-Impact Practices, especially writing, undergraduate research, and service-learning.

Rusty involves undergraduate and graduate student scholars in all of his research and publications. He considers it important for students to touch this work. Foremost, he never sends a publication out for review or to press without a student perspective. Many of our manuscripts will be read and even reviewed by highly talented student researchers. Students will often see issues and possibilities that we cannot. They have informed perspectives on current research trends. For example, Rusty recently coauthored a substantial book chapter with a graduate student focused on design issues in research posters. Her research interests and experiences in visual communication, paired with his own experience leading presentations on design in the communication process and years of experience teaching students to create research posters, made the ideal complement. In another case, Rusty is collaborating with an undergraduate Honors student research team to examine student learning through the use of metacognitive strategies. The students and he present at major national conferences and have received invitations to submit publications to national and international venues.

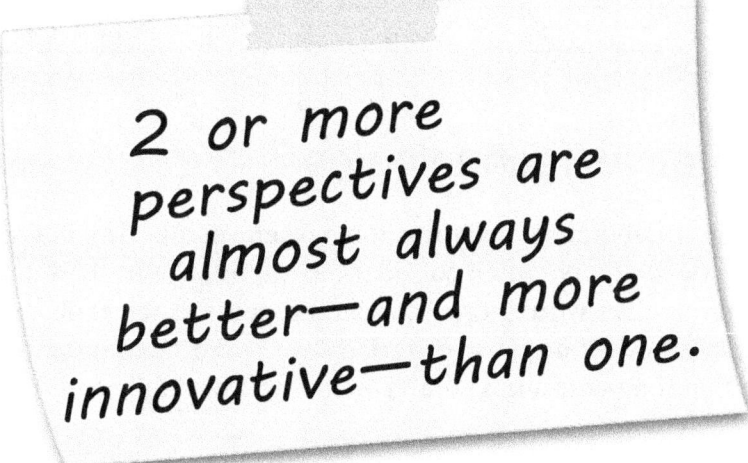

2 or more perspectives are almost always better—and more innovative—than one.

Bill has both mentored students on conference presentations and co-written SoTL pieces for peer-reviewed collections. Hal and Charlie have collaborated with students on chapters and bibliographies for several of their books.

Two for the price of one!

Graduate and undergraduate students in the Noel Studio – Teaching & Learning Center programs are viewed as co-researchers and collaborators, an important shift in thinking about the ways we organize our writing, research, and publication processes. It is rare that students are not involved in highly academic and rigorous ways in major research and publications generated in our program. While many graduate students work quietly behind the scenes, some are given specific writing and research assignments. Occasionally, some of these students have taken the initiative to submit proposals to us that later became collaborative publications.

Higher education institutions are being forced to adapt. Performance-based funding models and other incentives will force faculty to engage students in new ways. Moreover, the pressure to produce quality, timely scholarship suggests that we design major scholarly projects in concert with those we aim to educate. To that end, the education students receive in the process will continue to allow our institutions to adapt to meet the needs of scholarly and industry fields.

Table 2. Tracking Authorship

Type of Project	*Title*	*Author 1*	*Author 2*	*Author 3*	*Additional Authors*

Collaborative Technologies

We use many collaborative electronic tools when coauthoring major academic projects. We do not often consider the importance of these tools in ensuring a productive writing or researching process. **Such tools can reduce email traffic and increase productivity.** At the same time, these tools can ensure that time-consuming drafts are not lost or duplicated.

Table 3. Electronic Tools for Co-authorship

Tool	Description/Purpose	URL
Google Drive	Concurrent, collaborative drafting; cloud-based file storage, organization, and commenting	www.google.com/drive/
Dropbox	File storage and sharing; mass file transmittal	www.dropbox.com
Word	Track Changes	

Conclusion

Currier needed Ives, Darwin could not have evolved his theories without Lyell, and Isaac Newton could not have seen further without "standing on the shoulder of giants." Obviously, we have found collaboration a strategy that has maximized our talents, but, since everyone does not have the necessary dispositions for working with others, you'll have to make the decision about where you wish to stand yourself.

XII. CHARTING YOUR WAY WITH MULTIPLES PROJECTS

As you plan your drafting process, consider management strategies a priority. We often overlook this aspect of the process in favor of the research and publication goals themselves. A management strategy can allow you to document and plan your process while managing multiple simultaneous writing projects.

Rationale

In your academic career, you'll likely have the opportunity to take on many writing projects. You'll have to prioritize the ones that are most critical to your success, but the biggest projects are not always the best or even weighted heaviest. This chapter provides suggestions and strategies for finding your way with multiple writing projects. In this chapter, you'll learn:

- Strategies for managing multiple publication projects,

- Ways in which you might prioritize writing projects,

- Approaches to understanding the weight and significance of writing projects, and

- Strategies for analyzing different types of writing projects.

In addition, we'll provide you with tools you can use to track and manage major and minor writing projects. These tools allow you to chart your projects in their different stages from inception to publication.

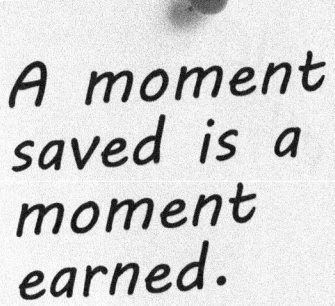

A moment saved is a moment earned.

Seven Charts In Search of an Author

As you develop a productive and complex scholarly agenda at your institution, reflecting on the stages of your publication projects takes on greater importance. **Understanding where these projects are in the publication process and how to move them forward to the next stage can allow you to manage your time better.** Many productive scholars have projects in each stage of the process, which allows for some projects to move forward and provides you time to search for venues for other projects that were not accepted or advanced. Table 1 offers definitions of the stages of the publication process.

Table 1. Definitions of the Publication Process

Active Writing	currently in the early, middle, or late stages of the drafting process
Revision	full draft is complete and major edits have begun, usually involving structural issues
Final Edits	full draft is substantially revised, line-level editing has begun
Publication and Proofing	publication has been accepted; publisher has provided copies of page proofs (often referred to as galley proofs); line level editing for correctness has begun

Let's start with an exercise. Use Table 2 to help you assess your current, planned, and future writing projects.

Table 2. Stages of the Writing Process

Writing Project	*Journal/Publication Venue*	*Stage*

Understanding the types of manuscripts available and how they might be classified or counted at your institution is important. Table 2 can assist the management process for your manuscripts.

What types of manuscripts are you currently authoring or co-authoring? Are you able to classify them into categories? Do you understand how your institution weights these publications? Table 3 will give you an idea of how to go about this important process. Faculty members are often asked to analyze their publications and contributions. The outline in Table 3 will support you in this process, whether for annual review, cataloging contributions in your institution's publication system, or drafting promotion and tenure narratives.

One size does NOT fit all.

76 / *Scaling the Scholarship Mountain*

Table 3. Types of Manuscripts

Type	Length/Range	Substance
Scholarly Note	Brief; up to 2,500 words	Focus on a specific and focused issue; introduces a concept or strategy
Article	2,500 words +	Focus on a larger issue, presentation and analysis of data
Book Chapter	Usually 2,500 words +; can be 30 pages +	Focus on a larger issue, presentation and analysis of data; usually focused on a related theme or issue
Edited Collection	Chapter lengths and number of chapters can vary	You cultivate the work of other authors, usually experts in the field; editors often write substantial introductions and conclusions that frame this scholarly work
Guest Edited Special Issue of Journal	Article lengths can vary; number of submissions can vary	You cultivate the work of other authors, usually experts in the field; guest editors usually also write introductions
Coauthored Book	Book lengths can vary; single-authored books are often over 100 pages in length	Coauthored books are often weighted heavily in the publication process, depending on the quality and reputation of the publisher
Single-authored Book	Book lengths can vary; coauthored books are often over 100 pages in length	Single-authored books are often held in the highest regard due to their commitment of time and the rigor of the review process, depending on the quality and reputation of the publisher

You will want to consider developing a strategy when submitting, revising, and finalizing major and minor manuscripts. Due dates, timelines, and publisher expectations will vary throughout the academic year. Some publishers will provide authors with rigid deadlines that must be met for the publication to remain on schedule.

Journal articles are likely the most common type of publication and will vary most widely depending on the journal or venue. Journals often review manuscripts related to their field on a rolling basis, meaning that you are welcome to submit when your manuscript is ready. Determining its potential for publication can be difficult, however. As expectations for publication increase, journals have become more selective. Some of the most competitive journals in different fields have single-digit acceptance rates and long turnaround times from initial review to decision to publication. Submitting to the top journal(s) in your field might be a good idea, but they're not always the ideal home for your work. **Assess the available and appropriate journals in your field for your manuscript's suitability.** Sometimes a selective, mid-tier journal can provide the best fit while offering you a reputable venue. In other cases, regional journals can give you the readership your manuscript needs.

Table 4. Journal Assessment

Manuscript Title	Stage	Journal Title	Journal Acceptance Rate	International, National, Regional, Local

Assessing book chapter authorship opportunities can be a bit more nuanced and challenging. In some cases, you might respond to an appealing call for papers or proposals (CFP), in which case your submission will be reviewed alongside others. Chapter proposal submissions can be highly competitive based on the editors and publisher. In some cases, however, the editors might invite a submission, in which case it is possible that they have a pre-planned table of contents prepared and expect your piece to fulfill a specific perspective within the book. While chapters count as a major publication, the peer-review process differs from editor and publisher to editor and publisher. Chapters selected for inclusion in books published by major university presses, while weighted heavily, can also take time to see in print.

Book manuscripts and edited collections take time as well. Securing a major book contract is more challenging now than it was even five years ago. University presses require complex review processes and multiple outside reviews before contracting. The review process can take a year or longer, depending on the popularity and volume of the publisher.

For every article, there is a journal.

Identifying potential book publication venues can be challenging. Not all manuscripts need to be submitted to major university presses. Your work might be best suited for major academic presses not affiliated with universities. **The first step in the process is usually composing a tightly written and compelling prospectus, a proposal that outlines your plans for the book, including your rationale, any research, and competition.** If your manuscript is not accepted from the beginning, you might decide to shop it around to multiple publishers before making a decision. The same is true for edited collections. Not all publishers invite proposals for these two types of manuscripts. It is important to assess these publication venues before beginning the process of submitting your prospectus.

Table 5 will give you an idea of how to manage the prospectus submission process. It is critical to have a clear idea of the books these publishers have released in recent years. Questions to consider include:

- What type of manuscript is this? Does the publisher invite this type of manuscript? (Single author vs multiple author; edited collection)

- Is the publisher actively inviting manuscripts?

- What is the typical time to publication?

- What is the review process for this publisher and how will you know the status of your manuscript?

Table 5. Managing the Prospectus Process

Book Title (prospectus)	Publisher's Prospectus Requirements	What titles has the publisher released similar to the one you've proposed?	What type of manuscript is it? Does the publisher invite this type of manuscript?

You must make your case strongly.

For books that include numerous chapters or edited collections, you must ensure that you are aware of the status of those pieces, especially when collaborating with colleagues or other editors. Table 6 will help you organize multiple submissions.

Table 6. Managing the Chapter and Editing Process

Chapter #	Chapter Title	Author(s)	Review 1	Review 2	Review 3	Final Editing

Managing and prioritizing manuscript writing and revision are not always a clear or clean process. Venue selectivity and prestige vary. A brief article featured in *Science*, for example, can outweigh books published with minor and lesser-known venues. We encourage you to analyze and prioritize these possibilities while also checking in with your institution to ensure that you are on track for success given your faculty priorities. Table 7 will help you track and prioritize projects at your institution.

Table 7. Tracking and Prioritizing Writing Projects

Type of Manuscript	Title	Status of Submission	Date Submitted	Editor/ Publisher Confirmed Receipt (Date)	Expected Review Decision	Priority Based on Institutional Expectations (1-5) – 1 – high/5 - low

Conclusion

As you begin your scholarly climb, management strategies might seem relatively unimportant. In this chapter, however, we've tried to show not only the significance of the strategies to your success, but also several protocols for extracting the maximum benefit from your time and effort while ensuring precise mentoring of your work. If you utilize the various suggestions and tables we provide, you'll be able to build your "scholarly muscles" over time so as to be capable of controlling your climb in an orderly fashion.

XIII. OVERCOMING OTHER OBSTACLES

Remember Bill's story about the two novice climbers who made their assent without proper preparation only to find themselves confronting a chasm without enough rope to traverse it? Even with their last-minute improvisation, one of them didn't survive. Likewise, in your attempt to scale the scholarship mountain, you will encounter additional obstacles, some for which you can plan before you start your climb; others, to which you'll have to react "on the fly." The major obstacles fall into five categories: over-commitment (the so-called "pancaked professor"), extreme esteem, rejectionslipitis, predatory publishing, and form difficulties (e.g., grammar, style, documentation).

Over-commitment

Whether you are new to teaching or a seasoned veteran, you are acutely aware of the demands on time and energy brought on by the profession. As we pointed out earlier, classes constitute only a portion of these demands (and less at an R1), even considering class preparation and grading in addition to the actual classroom/online presentation. Today's teacher is expected to exert both time and energy in service to the department, college, university, profession, and community. Consider for a moment—if you can free up one moment amidst your hectic schedule—just how much time and effort you expend in a normal week on committee work, office hours, completion of mandated paperwork, and professional development, and that portion of your life doesn't even take into account the demands of social (online and on-ground) and family life outside the university.

You are the captain of your (scholar)ship.

Then you're called on—and/or desire—to obtain scholarly productivity!

Our chapter on scholarly discipline offers a solid strategy for overcoming the over-commitment obstacle. **Carving out time and reserving the energy necessary for effective scholarly productivity take a concerted effort on your part.** Rather than trying to "sneak in" a moment here and there to work on your scholarship, you must set priorities and establish a workable schedule that will allow you to focus on your scholarship with minimal distractions. And you must have the discipline to follow through on your plan.

One of Hal and Charlie's mentors, the noted mystery author John D. MacDonald, told them that five days a week he spent the entire morning closeted in his office on the second floor of his house. His understanding wife, Dorothy, held sway on the first floor, making sure that nothing and nobody disturbed his productive time (it's probably a good thing social media and email hadn't been invented). And while Hal and Charlie could never match that discipline or that of long-time Hollywood screenwriter, Jack Sowards (e.g., *Star Trek: The Wrath of Khan*), who actually rented an office in downtown L.A. to which he retreated each day to write, they spent over 20 years writing two hours/day at a booth in a local McDonald's. Talk about a place to capture ideas.

When Bill retired from administration, he selected an office in a building on campus that has virtually no traffic, no interruptions, and near solitude in which to write. Because he teaches online, his office hours now become his writing time.

The point is: the remedy for over-commitment is discipline and a willingness to prioritize your scholarly productivity over those oftentimes valuable, but distracting activities that vie for your attention. As we point out in "The Pancake Professor and the Decline of Scholarly Writing" in the *Journal of Faculty Development* (2015), each year professors are stretched thinner and thinner by increasing demands, "flattening them out so they must do many things, and doing them well becomes an impossibility" (p. 70).

Extreme Esteem

We spoke earlier of a study that found 90% of all college teachers placed themselves in the top 10% in teaching effectiveness. Unfortunately, this type of self-deception can present another obstacle to your scholarly productivity. Too often, we have encountered newly-minted teachers who, fresh from successful stints in graduate school, believe that they can achieve publication as easily as they racked up As on their seminar papers. With degrees declaring them experts in their discipline, they often come to us eager to share their brilliant insights with the world.

Over their years as faculty developers, Hal and Charlie have been constantly accosted by young colleagues who are nonplussed when an editor has rejected a chapter from their dissertation that they submitted *in toto*. The guys have spent long hours with these would-be scholars, not only calming tempers but also working to modify the original to fit the needs of a suitable journal.

Just this morning, for example, we read an article which we strongly suspect came from a dissertation and was submitted to a journal on faculty development for a special issue on high-impact practices. Unfortunately,

> Take a few minutes to review.

the article never mentioned high-impact practices and had obviously tried to super-glue sections about faculty development that revealed a lack of knowledge about what faculty developers do. On top of that, the article offered no evidence (other than the old reliable in the humanities, quotes from other writers) to assert what helps students. A good study would have been a best practice, but that addition to the article necessitates the ability to create a study.

At the other end of the spectrum are the teachers—sometimes experienced colleagues—desiring to take the first or additional steps toward effective scholarly productivity, but feeling inadequate for the task. Most times new faculty are enthusiastic about the prospects afforded by the scholarly life and are eager to join the conversation. Although they are understandably a bit hesitant to put themselves and their work "out there" for review, such individuals are much easier to mentor than those colleagues who have tried unsuccessfully to see their work in print. Like the climber who has taken a fall, these people are wary of attempting another assault on Mount Scholarship.

Regardless of which of these camps best describes you—and we hope you align with neither—**the best way to avoid an esteem obstacle is to review our chapter on scholarly discipline and put its protocols into practice.** A hall-of-fame basketball coach was known for his insistence on his players developing an "honest respect" for every opponent, never fearing the confrontation, but always acknowledging the other teams' abilities and capacity for victory. So, too, should any faculty member wishing to successfully ascend the scholarship mountain develop a healthy respect for the difficulty involved without fearing the attempt.

Rejectionslipitis

When mountain climbers choose to conquer peaks in foreign lands, they often must visit their doctor to receive protective inoculations. Having ourselves written for years as well as working with faculty members wishing to succeed in scaling the alien heights of scholarly productivity, we have encountered a particularly debilitating malady that can sidetrack would-be scholars regardless of their self-esteem—or relative ability. What is especially pernicious about this illness is the fact that with each occurrence it seems to grow stronger, sometimes even causing an individual to abandon the scholarly climb.

Fortunately, years ago we discovered, not a painful inoculation, but a proven prescription to help you defeat the effects of what we call **rejectionslipitis, a debilitating mental condition that manifests as the inability to deal with rejection beyond inertia and leads to not only a work stoppage but a negative attitude toward productivity.**

The first step in the treatment calls on would-be scholars to change their attitude about rejection. We learned long ago that to write, to put your ideas out there for critical review, is to risk rejection. Sometimes that rejection can be harsh. Earlier Hal and Charlie recounted the story of their rather iconoclastic article on Robert Browning's "My Last Duchess," but they didn't tell the entire tale. On their first submission—to a rather snooty journal—they received a rejection along with one reviewer's stinging comment, "With names like Blythe and Sweet, this article must be some kind of joke." Bent but not broken, they confidently sent the piece off to an even more prestigious journal—where it was accepted. Sometimes a new route to publication has to be discovered. On a recent climb, Bill found a hidden land bridge across an abyss that saved him hours of laborious climbing.

Hal and Charlie's story is not unique, even to them. As we pointed out in the chapter on market research, they attempted breaking into the *Ellery Queen's Mystery Magazine* 20-plus times before success. If you wish to scale the scholarship mountain, you must first outfit yourself with layers of protective clothing since the climb, though rewarding, is not for the thin-skinned.

After recovering from the inevitable initial shock of a rejection slip, you can take the next step in our protocol by studying the rejection to see if it offers helpful information. If the editor says simply something such as "This does not meet our current needs," or you're presented with a small box checked "Reject," take heart in knowing that the rejection may not be a comment on the quality of your piece. The journal might be currently backlogged with accepted articles, it may have recently published a similar piece, or your article may fail to meet the journal's requirements for content, length, and style. Remember how we earlier stressed the importance of knowing the journal to which you submit.

Prepare for this debilitating disease with some strong medicine!

Sometimes an editor will include their reviewers' comments with the rejection. Study these critiques closely to see if they offer constructive information that might help you strengthen the piece. Since correspondence is now almost exclusively electronic, editors are more likely to comment personally on your article even if the decision is to reject, and these comments can be even more beneficial, often suggesting ways to make future submissions more attractive. As editor of the *Journal of Faculty Development*, Rusty has been known to go through more than five rounds of revise and resubmit with authors whose articles demonstrate promise. What most writers don't realize is articles can have multiple levels of problems, and each time one level is cleaned up, another problem is suddenly made visible. As a result, authors must be willing to endure the long process toward publication when at times it seems ridiculous to them.

Furthermore, you can enhance the effect of our prescription by submitting multiple pieces. It's much easier to tell yourself after a particularly heart-stabbing rejection, "Yes, but I still have nine other irons in the fire." Nine items makes one's emotional attachment to each piece a little less.

Once you have gleaned all you can from the rejection and made any revisions you think will strengthen the piece, send it out again. **Remember: no article was ever published sitting in your computer.** Keeping your article in circulation may be the most important step in our prescription for rejectionslipitis. Even if the article is rejected several additional times, with each stop you have a possibility of picking up valuable advice for the piece as well as future articles.

Rejectionslipitis doesn't have to be fatal; and, as the old saw says, "What doesn't kill me, makes me stronger."

Predatory Publishing

The term "predatory publishers" was coined by University of Colorado Denver librarian and researcher Jeffrey Beall, who developed 52 criteria to identify potential, possible, or probably open-access journals that exist less to spread knowledge than to siphon researchers' funds into their coffers. New professors, desperate for a publication who are willing to pay to play, seem most susceptible to this con. Among Beall's tell-tale signs are such items as quick acceptance, little or no time for peer review, notification of fees only after acceptance, journal names similar to those of real journals, and fake or non-existent impact factors. According to Beall, the number of such journals rose from a mere 18 in 2011 to an astonishing 923. Foreign authors, especially those in the sciences, appear to be most at risk. According to a recent study, Straumsheim (2015) claims such journals "dumped more than 420,00 articles into the market in 2014, up from 53,000 in 2010.

To combat this blight on academic publishing, Basken (2016) reports that in August 2016, the U.S. Federal Trade Commission filed suit in federal court in Nevada against one of the biggest publishers of online scientific journals, India-based OMICS Group, Inc. When Basken contacted Ioana Rusu, a staff attorney in the Bureau of Consumer Protection at the FTC, she said winning the case isn't as important as awakening academics who "aren't awfully aware of how far and wide this [abuse] goes." When Straumsheim (2016) asked Beall why he does his investigate work, the librarian-researcher responded, "Research published in predatory journals is polluting the entire scholarly publishing ecosystem."

And taking quite a few dollars from scholars hungry for publication.

Form Difficulties

Over the last few years, in our roles as editors of the *It Works for Me* series for New Forums as well as editing academic journals and judging proposals for an international conference hosted by our university, we have been struck by the level of writing crossing our desks. Certainly, this degeneration of both style and mechanics results from a number of factors, a major one being those pressures that create the "Pancake Professor" we mentioned earlier in the chapter. Regardless of the causes, however, the outcome is definite, and it serves as a major obstacle to successful scholarly productivity. Like the climber who comes to the mountain devoid of proper training in the basics of mountaineering, too many would-be scholars attempt scholarship without a solid mastery of the basics of grammar, style, and documentation.

While this book is not the proper venue for training in Writing 101, we will take this opportunity to advise you to hone your writing skills or risk immediate rejection of your scholarly material. When Rusty receives a submission for the *Journal of Faculty Development*, for instance, he gives it a reading **before** he sends it out for blind peer review. If the piece is poorly written or filled with errors in mechanics or documentation, Rusty doesn't send it forward.

Regardless of how insightful a piece may be, if it doesn't make its case clearly, it is of little value. Hal's brother-in-law was formerly the chief engineer at TRW, writing grants worth billions of dollars. He once complained to Hal that his most trying issue was finding engineers who could express themselves clearly in writing. Their ideas were game changing, but too often they could not communicate these ideas, even in inter-office memos, let alone multi-million-dollar grants.

One of the greatest advantages of collaboration is having more than one set of eyes to review writing before submission. Even then, as the four of us have discovered to our chagrin, errors slip through. As we stated earlier, we are not advocating perfection. We are, however, calling on you, whether you work alone or in collaboration, to make friends with one of the many handbooks out there and use it to produce the cleanest manuscript possible. **Don't allow the slippery slopes of style, mechanics, or documentation to hinder your assent of the scholarship mountain.**

In our pancake professor piece, we provide an error frequency chart—i.e., a list of "some of the most common problems we've discovered in scholarly writing" (pp. 69-70). Rather than quote *Hodges' Harbrace Handbook* or some other grammar guide, here are some common errors of which you need to be aware:

Strength through experience.

- Ambiguous references (e.g., "This is not the proper way to conduct an assessment" and "All of these are important")

- Lack of noun-pronoun agreement (e.g., "If an instructor . . . they")

- Mispunctuation of sentences with coordinating conjunctions (e.g., "I seized the opportunity, and gave an assessment" and "I went to class, so that I could study their behavior")

- Redundancies (e.g., "the reason why is because")

- Improper use of pronouns (e.g., "Theresa was the kind of student that took tests poorly")

- Failure to hyphenate two consecutive modifiers (e.g., "I developed a six minute video on degree completion students" or "low impact study")

- Wrongly setting off restrictive clauses with commas (e.g., "The students, that I found worked best, are those")

- Lack of subject-verb agreement (e.g., "After the final exam were taken," "Flipping my classroom have changed," and "The use of case studies are common")

- Lack of introductory commas (e.g., "Therefore I conclude flipping goes well")

- Improper use of apostrophe (e.g., "assess each students' understanding" and "each test has it's weakness)

- Faulty adverb placement (e.g., "Students only have one class to attend on Wednesdays")

- Modification errors (e.g., "Once completed, the groups discussed their findings").

Documentation

From the earliest days of high school, students are taught that documentation for any research project is **important**. As the student moves through undergraduate and graduate school, proper attribution of sources becomes ever more **necessary**. When doing research for publication at the professorial level, one quickly realizes that full and accurate documentation is **essential**.

Indeed, **the proper use of documentation is the mark of the scholar.**

Unfortunately, achieving expertise in scholarly documentation becomes more difficult with each passing year. Not only do the style and format differ across the disciplines, but within a given discipline changes may occur with little or no notice. For example, between the conception of this book and the writing of this chapter, MLA issued a 2016 update in our original field, English.

As a result, any attempt to treat proper form here would be futile. Rather, we'd like to offer a few guidelines that will help you conquer the obstacle, regardless of your discipline or scholarly interest.

1. Study the journal for which you want to write. In addition to analyzing the market, learn that publication's preferred (make that **demanded**) documentation style. Even though you might find yourself writing exclusively for journals using the same format, you might at times wish to venture into other areas of study. In the last year, for instance, we have published in three journals using three totally different documentation styles.

2. Become familiar with the handbooks, online sites, and software that provide guidance and realize that the material is in almost constant flux.

3. Once you have identified the journal's called-for style, be sure you follow it precisely, including your use of internal documentation and explanatory notes. When we edit submissions for the *Journal of Faculty Development* or for one of our "It Works for Me" collections, one of our most time-consuming and frustrating tasks is "cleaning up" shoddy documentation. We have, in fact, rejected submissions with poor documentation, feeling that such carelessness in preparation indicates a less-than-scholarly effort for the entire piece.

4. When in doubt, document! Oftentimes, source material that you gather might fall into the category of "general knowledge" (e.g., famous events, dates, events, personages, or quotes) not needing documentation even though you may have pulled it from a specific source. For instance, while doing an article on Viking conquests, you might have discovered that Odin's wife was Freya in Edith Hamilton's *Mythology*. Even though you didn't know this fact before reading Hamilton, it is such a well-known part of Norse mythology, you don't need to document your source. If, however, during your

By their references ye shall know them.

research, you encounter a scholar's theory on the relationship of Freya worship to the founding of the first Viking voyages to North America, you must credit your source.

5. When quoting borrowed material, meld it with your words smoothly:

- MLA: Mary Smith claims that "Freya had little impact on the early voyages of Eriksson to Canada around A.D. 1000" (35).

- APA: Smith (2016) claims, "Freya worship had little impact on the early voyage of Eriksson to Canada around A.D. 1000" (p. 35).

Conclusion

Whether its over-commitment, extreme esteem, rejectionslipitis, predatory publishers, form difficulties, or documentation, you must be aware and overcome any obstacle that impedes your assent of the scholarship mountain.

References

Basken, P. (2016, September 9). Federal prosecutors join the fight against predatory journals. *The Chronicle of Higher Education.* A15.

Straumsheim, C. (2015, October 1). Study finds huge increase in articles published by `predatory' journals. *Inside Higher Ed.* Retrieved from https://www.insidehighered.com/print/news/2015/10/01/study-finds-huge-increase-articles-published-by-pedatory-journals/.

Straumsheim, C. (2016, August 29). Federal trade commission begins to crack down on `predatory' publishers. *Inside Higher Ed.* Retrieved from https://www.insidehighered.com/print/news/2016/08/29/federal-trade-commission-begins-to-crack-down-on-predatory-publishers/.

Sweet, C., Carpenter, R., & Blythe, H. (2015). The pancake professor and the decline of scholarly writing. *Journal of Faculty Development*, 29(3), 69-70.

XIV. A CHECKLIST FOR STARTING YOUR SCHOLARLY PROJECT

One impulse in us wants to ask, why aren't you out there writing a scholarly piece for publication right now? Still another tells us by reading this book you are researching the entire publication process. Since you are about ready to begin, we're going to ask one more thing of you. In our *Achieving Excellence in Teaching* (2014), we provided a series of charts that allowed you to evaluate both your dispositions toward and strategies for teaching. Here, we are going to offer you a project checklist that begins with an inventory of scholarship skills we have discussed before moving into an actual research project. Whether you are beginning your initial ascent of the scholarship mountain or preparing for another attempt after previous struggles, our checklist should provide a systematic plan for success.

PROJECT CHECKLIST
1. Inventory of Pre-Project Skills

Directions: Evaluate yourself as to your attitude toward the following skills.

Scale: 1=All of the time, 2= Some of the time, 3=Rarely, 4=Never.

A. Desire for Scholarly Productivity (Intro-Chapter III)

_____ **Clarity**: I use writing and research to clarify my scholarly ideas.

_____ **Motivation**: I am motivated to produce scholarship intrinsically more than extrinsically.

_____ **Expertise**: I want to engage in 10,000 hours of writing.

_____ **Deep Learning**: I want to become a deep learner.

_____ **Academic Survival**: I wish to achieve tenure and promotion to the highest rank possible, even to carving out my own scholarly niche.

B. Scholarly Frame of Mind (Chapter IV)

_____ **Curiosity**: I am spurred on by my curious mind.

_____ **Active Answer-Seeker**: I actively seek answers and solutions to academic problems.

_____ **Rigor**: I possess and apply a series of skills necessary to pursue scholarly questions.

_____ **Discipline**: I am disciplined enough to produce scholarship on a regular basis at a regular time in a regular place with a goal.

_____ **Scholarly Conversation**: I am willing to join the scholarly conversation.

_____ **Excellence**: I am guided by excellence in my scholarly pursuits.

C. Taking Inventory (Chapter V)

_____ **On the Job I**: I sift through every day's events for germs for scholarly productions.

_____ **On the Job II**: On a daily basis I maintain and contribute to a file of ideas for scholarly productions.

_____ **Pre-Project Total Score**: Your PPTS is achieved by adding up your scores on each of the thirteen preceding statements. Obviously, the closer you are to 52, the less your desire to be a publishing scholar. No, we're not going to provide you with a scale a la popular magazines (e.g., 48-52=you are great), but we will suggest that to reach that goal, over time you need to improve any score more than 13.

2. Starting the Project

Directions: This section asks not that you evaluate your scholarly attitudes and habits, but rather provides a checklist for an actual scholarly production.

*A Caveat: Do not feel you must follow this systematic process exactly for every project you write (heck, we don't), but if you proceed through the checklist step-by-step, you **will** produce a solid scholarship artifact.*

Condition: At any point in the process, you may decide to collaborate. If so, consider our pronouns plural.

_____ 1. Select a germ from your idea file.

_____ 2. Decide which of Boyer's categories best describes your intentions with your idea.

_____ 3. Find a journal that you believe allows for the best expression of your idea and analyze that journal.

_____ 4. Develop a rough outline that follows the preferred format in the journal you selected.

_____ 5. Perform the research necessary for a literature review on your idea.

_____ 6. Draft an **Introduction** that centers around your thesis, hypothesis, or central question.

_____ 7. Draft a literature review that includes current, relevant, and sufficient sources that support your main idea.

_____ 8. Develop your **Body** of evidence, whether it comes from a study/survey (quantitative, qualitative) you perform, an analysis of a central artifact, or a conversation with your sources.

_____ 9. Create a satisfactory **Conclusion** that ties together your main idea and your evidence as well as performing other functions your format demands (e.g., limitations of your study, future research).

_____ 10. Combine your Introduction, Body, and Conclusion into a coherent draft.

_____ 11. Circulate the draft among friends. Consider using it as the basis of a conference presentation.

_____ 12. Revise the draft in accordance with suggestions you have received. Recirculate. Revise.

_____ 13. Send your completed version to the market you have analyzed.

_____ 14. Start all over again, keeping a record of your multiple works.

About the Authors

Charlie Sweet, Ph.D. (Florida State University, 1970), is the Co-Director of the Teaching & Learning Center at Eastern Kentucky University. With Hal, he has collaborated on over 1,200 published works, including 25 books, literary criticism, educational research, and novels (as Quinn MacHollister).

Hal Blythe, Ph.D. (Louisville, 1972), is the Co-Director of the Teaching & Learning Center. With Charlie, he has collaborated on over 1,200 published works, including 25 books (eight in New Forums' popular It Works For Me series), literary criticism, educational research, and a stint as ghostwriter of the lead novella for the *Mike Shayne Mystery Magazine*.

Russell Carpenter, Ph.D. (University of Central Florida, 2009), is Executive Director of the Noel Studio for Academic Creativity and Program Director of Applied Creative Thinking at Eastern Kentucky University where he is also Associate Professor of English. Dr. Carpenter has published on the topic of creative thinking, among other areas, including three texts by New Forums Press: *Introduction to Applied Creative Thinking* (with Charlie Sweet and Hal Blythe, 2012), *Teaching Applied Creative Thinking* (with Charlie Sweet, Hal Blythe, and Shawn Apostel, 2013), and *It Works for Me, Flipping the Classroom: Shared Tips for Effective Teaching*, (with Hal Blythe and Charlie Sweet, 2015). He has guest edited or co-edited special issues of the *Journal of Faculty Development* on social media and the future of faculty development, and now serves as the journal's editor. In addition, he has taught courses in creative thinking in EKU's Minor in Applied Creative Thinking, which was featured in the *New York Times* in February 2014, and rhetoric and composition in the Department of English.

Bill Phillips, Ed.D., (University of Southern Mississippi, 1988), is former Dean of the College of Education at Eastern Kentucky University and a collaborator on *Achieving Excellence in Teaching*, 2014.